The Ultimate Travellers Guide To Turkey

PA BOOKS

Published by PA BOOKS, 2023.

While every precaution has been taken in the preparation of this book, the publisher assumes no responsibility for errors or omissions, or for damages resulting from the use of the information contained herein.

THE ULTIMATE TRAVELLERS GUIDE TO TURKEY

First edition. November 28, 2023.

Copyright © 2023 PA BOOKS.

ISBN: 979-8223465485

Written by PA BOOKS.

Also by PA BOOKS

Hogan's Key
Kimberly & the Five Strange Goldfishes
The Enchanted Library
The Misadventures of Pirate Pete
From Wheel To Web: 40 Remarkable Inventions
Once Upon A Sleepy Time
The Global Game - The Evolution Of Football
Strides To Success: A Beginner's Guide to Running
The ChatGPT Handbook
Climate Crossroads
1000 Everyday Life Hacks
Urban Exploration - London The Comprehensive Travel Guide
Urban Exploration - New York The Comprehensive Travel Guide
Urban Exploration - Amsterdam The Comprehensive Travel Guide
Urban Exploration - Barcelona The Comprehensive Travel Guide
Urban Exploration - Dubai The Comprehensive Travel Guide
Urban Exploration - Paris The Comprehensive Travel Guide
World Of Festivals - The Ultimate Guide
The Ultimate Travellers Guide To Turkey

Table of Contents

Introduction to Turkey: Where East Meets West.................................... 1

Historical Marvels: Exploring Ancient Ruins 3

Istanbul: Where East Meets West 7

Culinary Delights: A Feast for the Senses 11

Turkish Arts and Culture: A Tapestry of Tradition and Innovation ..15

Mediterranean Magic: The Turquoise Coast......................................21

Cappadocia: A Fairy Tale Landscape 27

Anatolian Adventures: Off the Beaten Path 33

Turkish Hospitality: Staying with Locals 39

Natural Wonders: National Parks and Landscapes 47

Practical Travel Tips: Navigating Language and Customs...................53

Festivals and Celebrations: Immersing in Local Traditions..................61

Adventure Seeker's Paradise: Outdoor Activities in Turkey................73

Shopping in Turkey: Souvenirs and Beyond....................................83

Modern Marvels: Turkey's Contemporary Scene 93

Getting Around: Transportation Tips in Turkey............................ 101

Health and Safety: Essential Guidelines for Traveling in Turkey..... 113

Planning Your Trip: Itinerary Suggestions for Every Travel Style.... 125

Conclusion: A Journey to Remember - Unveiling the Tapestry of Turkey's Charms.. 137

Introduction to Turkey: Where East Meets West

Turkey, a mesmerizing tapestry of cultures, landscapes, and history, invites travellers on a journey that transcends time and borders. Nestled at the crossroads of Europe and Asia, this transcontinental country is a mosaic of ancient ruins, vibrant bazaars, and breath-taking landscapes that stretch from the Aegean coast to the rugged Anatolian plateau.

Geography and Diversity:

Turkey's geographical allure is unparalleled. To the west, the azure waters of the Aegean Sea lap against the sun-soaked beaches, adorned with olive groves and ancient ruins. In contrast, the east boasts the arid beauty of Cappadocia, where otherworldly landscapes of fairy chimneys and cave dwellings punctuate the horizon. From the bustling metropolis of Istanbul, straddling the Bosphorus Strait, to the serene tranquillity of Pamukkale's terraces, Turkey's diversity is as vast as its history.

Rich History and Heritage:

Turkey's history is a tapestry woven with threads of empires, civilizations, and mythologies. Walk in the footsteps of ancient Romans at Ephesus, where the grandeur of the Library of Celsus and the Theatre evoke the echoes of the past. Discover the secrets of the underground cities in Cappadocia, witness the architectural marvel of Hagia Sophia in Istanbul, and explore the mystique of Troy, the legendary city of Homer's epics.

Modern Splendours:

Beyond its historical treasures, Turkey pulsates with a modern vibrancy. Istanbul, a city straddling two continents, marries the historic charm of the Grand Bazaar with the contemporary chic of Beyoğlu. Indulge in the rich flavours of Turkish cuisine, a tantalizing fusion of spices and culinary traditions that draw from Ottoman, Persian, and Mediterranean influences.

Warm Hospitality:

At the heart of Turkey's allure is the warmth of its people. Turkish hospitality, renowned worldwide, transforms a simple encounter into a cherished memory. Whether sipping tea in a quaint village or navigating the bustling alleys of the Grand Bazaar, the Turkish people's genuine friendliness leaves an indelible mark on every traveller's heart.

Practicalities and Travel Tips:

Navigating Turkey is a delightful challenge, and with a few practical tips, you can make the most of your journey. Understanding the local customs, embracing the diverse modes of transportation, and savouring the nuances of Turkish etiquette will enhance your travel experience.

Join us on a captivating exploration of Turkey, where ancient traditions dance with contemporary lifestyles, and where every step is a passage through time. "Ultimate Turkey - The Travel Guide" is your key to unlocking the treasures of this enchanting land, where East meets West in a harmonious blend of history, culture, and natural beauty.

Historical Marvels: Exploring Ancient Ruins

In the sun-drenched embrace of Turkey, where history whispers through the winds and the stones, the allure of ancient ruins beckons to those seeking a journey through time. As you tread upon the weathered paths of civilizations long past, immerse yourself in the awe-inspiring stories etched in the stones of iconic sites like Ephesus, Troy, and Hierapolis.

Ephesus: A Timeless Tapestry of Antiquity

Step into the ruins of Ephesus, a city frozen in time, where the echoes of Roman senators and Greek philosophers resonate through the marble columns and cobbled streets. The grandeur of Ephesus unfolds at the majestic Library of Celsus, an architectural marvel that once housed thousands of scrolls. Wander through the expansive Roman Agora, where the marketplace once bustled with merchants and traders from across the ancient world.

As you stand in the shadow of the Great Theatre, envision the performances that once captivated audiences in this colossal amphitheatre. Ephesus, once a thriving port city, invites you to traverse the remnants of the Terrace Houses, where the opulence of Roman aristocracy is preserved in exquisite frescoes and mosaic floors. Each stone in Ephesus whispers tales of the past, making it an essential pilgrimage for history enthusiasts.

Troy: Unravelling the Layers of Myth and Reality

Venture into the ancient land of Troy, where the mythical tales of Helen, Achilles, and the Trojan horse intertwine with archaeological wonders. The layers of Troy, each revealing a different epoch, unravel beneath your feet as you explore the city's nine ancient layers. Stand before the imposing walls of Troy VI, witness the remnants of sacrificial altars, and contemplate the enigma of the wooden horse in the archaeological site that spans millennia.

Troy, immortalized in Homer's "Iliad," invites you to contemplate the convergence of myth and history. Wander through the ruins of the city gate and imagine the clash of bronze-clad warriors beneath the looming walls. The archaeological site is a testament to the resilience of a city that rose and fell through the ages, leaving behind a legacy that captivates the imagination.

Hierapolis: A Sanctuary in the Heavens

Perched on the slopes of Pamukkale, the ancient city of Hierapolis transports you to a realm where history and natural wonders converge. Hierapolis, with its striking necropolis and well-preserved theatre, is a testament to the city's prominence in the Hellenistic and Roman periods. The Sacred Pool, fed by thermal springs, invites you to immerse yourself in rejuvenating waters, echoing the healing traditions of the ancients.

The white terraces of Pamukkale, resembling a cascade of frozen water, beckon you to wander barefoot on the travertine terraces. As you explore the Temple of Apollo and the Plutonium, a cave associated with the god of the underworld, you'll feel the spiritual aura of this ancient sanctuary. Hierapolis, a UNESCO World Heritage Site, offers not only archaeological wonders but also breath-taking views of the landscape below.

Practical Tips for Exploring Ancient Ruins:

- Guided Tours: Consider joining guided tours at these historical sites to gain in-depth insights into their history and significance.

Knowledgeable guides can provide context and bring the ruins to life with captivating stories.

- Comfortable Footwear: The terrain in ancient ruins can be uneven, so wear comfortable and sturdy footwear to navigate the archaeological sites with ease.

- Sun Protection: Turkey's sun can be intense, especially during the summer. Don't forget to bring sunscreen, a hat, and sunglasses to stay protected while exploring.

- Water and Snacks: Stay hydrated during your explorations by carrying a water bottle. Packing some snacks is also advisable, as you may spend several hours immersed in the rich history of these sites.

Embark on a journey through the remnants of ancient civilizations, where every stone tells a story and every step is a communion with the past. The historical marvels of Ephesus, Troy, and Hierapolis await, inviting you to uncover the mysteries and wonders of Turkey's profound heritage.

Istanbul: Where East Meets West

In the heart of Turkey, at the crossroads of two continents, lies a city that encapsulates the essence of cultural fusion—Istanbul. This metropolis, straddling the Bosphorus Strait, is a living testament to the confluence of East and West, where ancient traditions coexist with a vibrant modernity. Navigating the streets of Istanbul is a sensory journey, an exploration of historical treasures, culinary delights, and the pulse of a city that has been a capital of three great empires.

The Tapestry of Istanbul:

As the sun rises over the Bosphorus, Istanbul awakens, a city steeped in history and wrapped in the tapestry of diverse influences. The cityscape is an eclectic mix of minarets, domes, and modern skyscrapers, creating a skyline that reflects its multifaceted identity. The silhouette of the Hagia Sophia and the Blue Mosque against the changing hues of the sky is a visual symphony that encapsulates the spirit of Istanbul.

Hagia Sophia: A Divine Marvel Transformed

The Hagia Sophia, a cultural marvel that has witnessed the ebb and flow of empires, stands as a testament to Istanbul's rich history. Originally constructed as a cathedral in the 6th century, it later became a mosque under Ottoman rule and, in recent times, has been repurposed as a museum. The Hagia Sophia is a living chronicle of Istanbul's journey through different epochs, with its stunning mosaics, massive dome, and awe-inspiring architecture.

As you step into the Hagia Sophia, you're transported to a realm where Byzantine and Ottoman influences converge. Marvel at the intricate details of the mosaics, depicting religious scenes and imperial figures, and stand beneath the colossal dome that seems to touch the heavens.

The Hagia Sophia, a UNESCO World Heritage Site, is a must-visit, inviting you to witness the layers of history woven into its walls.

Blue Mosque: A Spiritual Oasis

Adjacent to the Hagia Sophia, the Blue Mosque, or Sultan Ahmed Mosque, unfolds its grandeur like a celestial oasis. Adorned with cascading domes and six slender minarets, the mosque earned its nickname from the blue tiles that embellish its interior. Step into the courtyard, where the rhythmic sound of fountains accompanies the mesmerizing sight of the mosque's domes reaching towards the sky.

The interior of the Blue Mosque is a symphony of blue and gold, with intricate tile work and calligraphy adorning the walls. The central dome, supported by majestic columns, creates an ethereal ambiance that invites contemplation. As the sunlight filters through the stained glass windows, the prayer area comes alive with a celestial glow. The Blue Mosque is not merely a place of worship; it's an architectural masterpiece that harmonizes spiritual and aesthetic elements.

Grand Bazaar: A Labyrinth of Treasures

No exploration of Istanbul is complete without delving into the labyrinthine lanes of the Grand Bazaar. A bustling marketplace that has stood for centuries, the Grand Bazaar is a kaleidoscope of colours, scents, and sounds. Navigating through its myriad alleys, you'll encounter a treasure trove of Turkish delights—spices, carpets, jewellery, and an array of unique artefacts that echo the craftsmanship of generations.

Engage in the art of haggling as you peruse the stalls, each laden with the allure of the Orient. The Grand Bazaar is not merely a shopping destination; it's an immersion into the cultural richness of Turkey. Sip traditional Turkish tea at a carpet shop, marvel at the intricacy of handmade ceramics, and lose yourself in the vibrant tapestry of this historical marketplace.

Navigating the Streets: Tips for Exploring Istanbul

- Public Transportation: Istanbul's traffic can be daunting, so utilize the efficient public transportation system. The tram is a convenient way to move between historical sites, and ferries offer a scenic route across the Bosphorus.

- Appreciating Local Cuisine: Istanbul is a gastronomic paradise. Don't miss the opportunity to savour kebabs, mezes, and Turkish sweets. Venture beyond the tourist spots to discover hidden gems where locals dine.

- Respecting Cultural Norms: While exploring Istanbul, dress modestly when visiting religious sites and be mindful of local customs. Engage with locals with a warm

"Merhaba" (hello) and embrace the cultural diversity around you.

- Bosphorus Cruise: Gain a unique perspective of Istanbul by embarking on a Bosphorus cruise. Witness the city's skyline shimmering against the water and marvel at the historic landmarks from a different vantage point.

Conclusion:

Istanbul, where East meets west, is a city that transcends time and captivates the soul. From the spiritual sanctuaries of the Hagia Sophia and the Blue Mosque to the vibrant tapestry of the Grand Bazaar, each step in Istanbul is a dance between tradition and modernity. As you navigate its streets, you'll find yourself immersed in a city that is not just a destination but an experience—an exploration of history, culture, and the timeless allure of a city that straddles two continents. Istanbul, with its harmonious blend of the ancient and the contemporary, invites you to become a part of its rich narrative, where every corner tells a story, and every encounter is a celebration of diversity.

Culinary Delights: A Feast for the Senses

In the heart of Turkey, where the aroma of spices dances in the air and the sizzle of grills serenades the streets, culinary delights become an integral part of the travel experience. Turkish cuisine, a harmonious blend of flavours and traditions, is a journey through history, geography, and the vibrant spirit of a nation. From succulent kebabs and tantalizing mezze to the sweet embrace of baklava and the comforting warmth of Turkish tea, each dish is a celebration of the rich tapestry that is Turkish gastronomy.

The Art of Mezze: A Symphony of Small Plates

Embark on a culinary odyssey with the quintessential Turkish tradition of mezze—a symphony of small plates that tantalize the palate and offer a glimpse into the diversity of Turkish flavours. Begin your mezze adventure with hummus, a creamy blend of chickpeas, tahini, and olive oil, adorned with a sprinkle of paprika. Dive into the smoky allure of baba ganoush, a roasted eggplant delight, and savour the tangy kick of cacik, a refreshing yogurt and cucumber dip.

The mezze table is a canvas of colours and textures, featuring stuffed grape leaves (dolma), fava bean puree, and muhammara, a roasted red pepper and walnut spread. As you navigate this culinary landscape, let the flavours tell the stories of the Mediterranean, Aegean, and Anatolian regions, each contributing its unique essence to the mezze tapestry.

Kebabs: A Grilled Symphony of Savoury Perfection

No exploration of Turkish cuisine is complete without indulging in the savoury delight of kebabs. The streets of Turkey echo with the sizzle of grills, and the aroma of marinated meats draws you to the myriad kebab joints that line the alleys. Sink your teeth into a succulent Adana kebab, a spicy minced meat skewer that hails from the south, or savour the simplicity of a shish kebab, where marinated chunks of meat are grilled to perfection.

For a taste of history, try the Iskender kebab, named after Alexander the Great, featuring thinly sliced lamb on a bed of pita bread, drenched in tomato sauce and yogurt. In Istanbul, the iconic street food known as döner kebab beckons, with layers of seasoned meat slowly roasted on a vertical spit, creating a mouth-watering combination of crisp edges and juicy tenderness.

Turkish Delight: The Sweet Symphony of Baklava

As the sun sets over the minarets, embark on a sweet journey with the crown jewel of Turkish desserts—baklava. Layers of thin pastry, generously buttered and layered with chopped nuts, are baked to golden perfection and then drenched in a sweet syrup, creating a symphony of textures and flavours that dance on the taste buds.

Whether enjoyed in a historic café in Istanbul or purchased from a bustling market, each bite of baklava is a celebration of the artistry that defines Turkish pastry-making. Varieties abound, from walnut-filled to pistachio-laden, offering a sweet finale to a Turkish feast.

Turkish Tea: The Warm Embrace of Tradition

In the midst of your culinary journey, pause to experience the warmth of Turkish tea—a ritual that transcends mere refreshment and serves as a symbol of hospitality and connection. Sipped from petite tulip-shaped glasses, Turkish tea is a daily tradition that invites conversation, relaxation, and a moment of respite.

Whether enjoyed at a street-side çayhane (tea house) or in the tranquil courtyard of a historic mosque, Turkish tea is an integral part of the social fabric. Pair it with a cube of sugar, a traditional gesture of sweetness, and let the soothing warmth of the tea envelop you as you soak in the rich atmosphere of Turkish culture.

Practical Tips for Culinary Exploration:

- Local Markets: Immerse yourself in the local food culture by exploring bustling markets like the Spice Bazaar in Istanbul. Engage with vendors, sample fresh produce, and discover the ingredients that form the foundation of Turkish cuisine.

- Regional Specialties: Turkey's diverse regions boast unique culinary specialties. Don't hesitate to try local dishes, from Black Sea seafood to South-eastern Anatolian stews. Each region offers a culinary adventure waiting to be savoured.

- Street Food Excursions: Embrace the vibrant street food scene, especially in cities like Istanbul. Try simit (sesame-covered bread rings), midye dolma (stuffed mussels), and kumpir (loaded baked potatoes) from street vendors for an authentic taste of Turkish street cuisine.

- Dining Etiquette: In Turkey, it's customary to greet your hosts with "Afiyet olsun" (May it be good for your health) before and after a meal. Embrace the communal spirit of dining by sharing dishes with fellow travellers and locals alike.

Embark on a sensory adventure through the culinary wonders of Turkey, where every dish is a brushstroke in a masterpiece that reflects the nation's rich history and cultural diversity. From the lively mezzes to the succulent kebabs, the sweet notes of baklava to the comforting embrace of Turkish tea, each flavour invites you to partake in a feast for the senses—an exploration that goes beyond the table and becomes a cherished memory of your journey through Turkey's gastronomic treasures.

Turkish Arts and Culture: A Tapestry of Tradition and Innovation

In the heart of Turkey, where history weaves itself into the fabric of everyday life, the arts and culture stand as living testaments to the nation's rich heritage. From the intricate designs of Turkish ceramics to the mesmerizing patterns of handmade carpets, Turkey's artistic traditions embody a synthesis of influences that have shaped the region over centuries. Join us on a journey through the vibrant tapestry of Turkish arts and culture, where each creation is a brushstroke in the portrait of a nation.

Ceramics: The Artistry of Iznik Tiles

Step into the world of Iznik ceramics, where tiles adorned with vibrant patterns transform spaces into works of art. Iznik, a town with a storied history in ceramic production, is renowned for its distinctive blue-and-white tiles that have graced the walls of mosques, palaces, and homes for centuries. The intricate designs, often featuring floral motifs and geometric patterns, reflect a synthesis of Ottoman, Persian, and Anatolian influences.

Visit the Rustem Pasha Mosque in Istanbul, a hidden gem adorned with Iznik tiles that narrate stories of nature, mythology, and daily life. The Topkapi Palace, once the seat of Ottoman power, showcases the grandeur of Iznik tiles in its Harem and Circumcision Room. As you explore these spaces, feel the artistry that emanates from each tile, telling tales of a bygone era.

Calligraphy: The Elegance of the Written Word

In the realm of Turkish arts, calligraphy stands as a revered tradition, where the written word becomes a visual symphony of elegance.

Turkish calligraphy, deeply rooted in Islamic culture, transcends mere writing to become a form of artistic expression. The sweeping curves and intricate details of Ottoman calligraphy transform verses from the Quran and poetic expressions into visual masterpieces.

Visit the Mevlana Museum in Konya, dedicated to the mystic poet Rumi, to witness the beauty of Ottoman calligraphy. The elegant strokes of the pen bring to life verses that transcend time, inviting contemplation and reflection. In Istanbul, explore the Calligraphy Museum within the Topkapi Palace, where the evolution of this art form is showcased through a collection of exquisite manuscripts.

Turkish Carpets: Woven Tales of Tradition

The art of carpet weaving in Turkey is a craft that has been passed down through generations, creating masterpieces that adorn both palaces and humble homes. Turkish carpets, known for their intricate patterns and vibrant colours, are woven with stories that reflect the cultural diversity of the regions where they are crafted. From the nomadic traditions of the Anatolian plateau to the coastal influences of the Aegean, each carpet tells a tale of its origin.

Explore the Grand Bazaar in Istanbul, a labyrinth of carpet shops where you can witness the craftsmanship first-hand. Feel the softness of hand-knotted silk carpets and admire the durability of woollen masterpieces. Each knot, each colour, is a brushstroke in a canvas that captures the essence of Turkish artistry.

Whirling Dervishes: Sufi Mysticism in Motion

The mesmerizing ritual of the Whirling Dervishes, also known as the Mevlevi Order, is a dance that transcends the boundaries of performance and becomes a spiritual journey. Rooted in Sufi mysticism, the whirling dance is a form of meditation, a ritual that seeks to achieve a union with the divine. The flowing white robes of the dervishes and the meditative trance of their dance create a mesmerizing spectacle.

Attend a Sema ceremony in Konya, the city of Rumi, to witness the spiritual grace of the Whirling Dervishes. The dance, accompanied by traditional music and chanting, is a window into the mystical traditions that have shaped Turkish spirituality. As the dervishes whirl in perfect harmony, it becomes a visual metaphor for the cosmic dance of the universe.

Music and Instruments: Harmonies of Anatolia

The music of Turkey is a rich tapestry that reflects the cultural diversity of the Anatolian region. From the haunting melodies of the ney (reed flute) to the rhythmic beats of the darbuka (goblet drum), Turkish music invites you to experience a symphony of sounds that resonate with history and emotion. Traditional folk music, classical Ottoman compositions, and contemporary tunes create a diverse musical landscape.

Explore the sounds of Istanbul at the Istanbul Music Festival, where world-class musicians gather to celebrate the harmonies of Anatolia. Visit the Aspendos International Opera and Ballet Festival, held in the ancient amphitheatre of Aspendos, to witness performances against the backdrop of ancient ruins. Whether it's the soul-stirring tunes of Turkish classical music or the vibrant beats of folk dances, the music of Turkey is a journey through time and emotion.

Practical Tips for Immersing in Turkish Arts and Culture:

- Artisan Workshops: Seek out artisan workshops where you can witness the creation of Turkish crafts first-hand. From ceramic studios in Iznik to carpet weaving cooperatives in Cappadocia, these workshops offer a deeper understanding of the artistic process.

- Cultural Festivals: Plan your visit around cultural festivals that showcase the arts of Turkey. The Istanbul Biennial, the International Istanbul Opera Festival, and the Konya Mystic Music Festival are just a few examples of events that celebrate Turkish culture.

- Local Museums: Explore local museums dedicated to Turkish arts. The Museum of Turkish and Islamic Arts in Istanbul, the Kariye Museum with its stunning mosaics, and the Mevlana Museum in

Konya are invaluable resources for delving into the country's artistic heritage.

- Interactive Experiences: Engage in interactive experiences, such as calligraphy workshops or dance performances, to connect with Turkish arts on a personal level. Local cultural centres often offer these opportunities for travellers seeking a hands-on experience.

Embark on a journey through the artistic and cultural wonders of Turkey, where every brushstroke, every note, and every knot tell stories of a nation deeply rooted in tradition yet embracing the winds of change. From the vibrant tiles of Iznik to the spiritual dance of the Whirling Dervishes, Turkish arts and culture invite you to become a part of a living tapestry—one that celebrates the beauty of diversity, the richness of history, and the timeless allure of creativity.

Mediterranean Magic: The Turquoise Coast

Along the south-western edge of Turkey unfolds a realm of enchantment—the Turquoise Coast. A stretch of coastline where the Aegean and Mediterranean Seas embrace, the Turquoise Coast is a symphony of azure waters, golden beaches, and ancient wonders. Join us on a journey along this captivating shoreline, where every cove, every ancient city, and every sailing adventure paints a portrait of Mediterranean magic.

Antalya: Gateway to the Turquoise Coast

As the sun-drenched gateway to the Turquoise Coast, Antalya beckons with its blend of modern luxury and ancient charm. The city, nestled between the Taurus Mountains and the glistening Mediterranean, is a fusion of turquoise waters and palm-lined boulevards. Begin your exploration in Kaleiçi, the historic quarter, where narrow cobblestone streets wind past Ottoman houses, boutique hotels, and vibrant markets.

Visit Hadrian's Gate, an iconic entrance to the city built to honour the Roman Emperor Hadrian. Wander through the Antalya Museum, home to artefacts from the region's rich history, including pieces from ancient cities along the coast. As the day unfolds, bask in the sunset glow at the Hıdırlık Tower, offering panoramic views of the harbour and the surrounding landscape.

Belek and Kemer: Golfer's Paradise and Resort Retreat

Venture east to Belek, a haven for golf enthusiasts. This coastal town boasts world-class golf courses set against a backdrop of pine forests and the Mediterranean Sea. Tee off with the sea breeze as your companion and savour the unique experience of golfing in the Turkish sunshine.

Continue west to Kemer, a resort town that balances modern amenities with the natural beauty of the Turquoise Coast. Relax on pristine beaches, explore the marina, and discover the vibrant nightlife that comes alive as the sun sets over the Mediterranean. Kemer is not only a gateway to sea adventures but also an oasis for those seeking relaxation and luxury.

Olympos: A Tapestry of Nature and History

As you travel along the Turquoise Coast, immerse yourself in the natural and historical tapestry of Olympos. Nestled between the mountains and the sea, Olympos is a haven for nature lovers and history enthusiasts alike. The ancient city, scattered with ruins dating back to the Hellenistic and Roman periods, unfolds amidst a landscape of pine forests and pebble beaches.

Explore the ancient theatre, the ruins of the Temple of Hephaestus, and the Roman bathhouse. Follow the path of the Lycian Way, a hiking trail that winds through the region, offering breath-taking views of the coastline. For a unique experience, visit the Chimera, where eternal flames flicker from vents in the rocky terrain—a phenomenon that has captivated travellers for centuries.

Phaselis: Ruins by the Sea

Continue your journey to Phaselis, an ancient Lycian city steeped in history and surrounded by pristine beaches. This archaeological gem invites you to wander through well-preserved ruins set against a backdrop of azure waters. The city, founded in the 7th century BCE, flourished as a maritime and trade centre.

Stroll along the grand avenue adorned with ancient columns, explore the ruins of the Roman bathhouse, and imagine the bustling port that once connected civilizations. Phaselis is a testament to the region's rich past, and its well-preserved harbour is an idyllic spot for a refreshing swim with the echoes of ancient mariners as your companions.

Kaş: Underwater Wonders and Coastal Charms

As you continue westward, the charming town of Kaş unfolds—a coastal paradise where vibrant bougainvillea cascades down whitewashed buildings and the scent of jasmine wafts through the air. Kaş is not only a picturesque destination but also a hub for underwater adventures.

Dive into the crystal-clear waters to explore underwater caves, vibrant coral reefs, and the sunken city of Kekova. The Lycian Way continues here, offering hiking enthusiasts a chance to traverse coastal trails with panoramic views. Explore the Lycian tombs carved into the cliffs, visit the ancient theatre, and savour freshly caught seafood in the welcoming ambiance of local restaurants.

Kekova: A Submerged History

Sailing along the Turquoise Coast reveals the submerged history of Kekova—an island where the ruins of an ancient city succumbed to the waters. The partially sunken city, dating back to the 2nd century BCE, offers a unique perspective on the interplay between nature and history.

Take a boat tour to witness the sunken remains of buildings, staircases, and walls beneath the clear waters of Kekova. Glide over the sunken city, and as the sunlight filters through the sea, let your imagination paint a picture of the thriving city that once stood here. The juxtaposition of ancient ruins and the tranquil beauty of the Mediterranean creates a scene that is both poignant and breath-taking.

Kaş to Fethiye: Sailing the Blue Voyage

Embark on a Blue Voyage, a sailing odyssey that captures the essence of the Turquoise Coast. Setting sail from Kaş to Fethiye, you'll traverse crystal-clear waters, explore hidden coves, and anchor at picturesque bays along the way. The Blue Voyage, inspired by Turkish author Cevat Şakir Kabaağaçlı, is a journey that combines the allure of sailing with the exploration of coastal treasures.

Drop anchor at Butterfly Valley, a secluded beach surrounded by steep cliffs and home to diverse flora and fauna. Hike up to the waterfall, swim in the azure waters, and let the natural beauty of the valley unfold before you. Continue to Ölüdeniz, renowned for its pristine Blue Lagoon, where shades of turquoise and azure create a palette that is nothing short of magical.

Fethiye: A Coastal Haven

As your journey along the Turquoise Coast culminates in Fethiye, you'll discover a coastal haven that seamlessly blends ancient history with modern charm. The city, built upon the ruins of the ancient Lycian city of Telmessos, invites you to explore the rock tombs that overlook the modern harbour.

Visit the Lycian sarcophagi scattered throughout the city and ascend to the ancient theatre for panoramic views of Fethiye and the surrounding coastline. The bustling harbour is adorned with waterfront restaurants, lively markets, and the imposing Fethiye Castle—a fortress that has stood sentinel over the bay for centuries.

Practical Tips for Exploring the Turquoise Coast:

- Blue Voyage Planning: If embarking on a Blue Voyage, plan your itinerary to include secluded coves, hidden beaches, and vibrant coastal towns. Many local operators offer sailing tours with various durations, allowing you to tailor the experience to your preferences.

- Hiking Adventures: The Lycian Way, one of the world's great long-distance hiking trails, offers unparalleled views of the Turquoise Coast. Plan hiking excursions to explore ancient ruins, witness breath-taking landscapes, and experience the coastal beauty from a different perspective.

- Local Cuisine: Indulge in the flavours of the Turquoise Coast by savouring seafood delicacies, fresh fruits, and regional specialties. Waterfront restaurants in Kaş, Fethiye, and other coastal towns offer a culinary journey that complements the coastal ambiance.

- Water Activities: Take advantage of the crystal-clear waters

For snorkelling, diving, and swimming. Many coastal towns, including Kaş and Fethiye, have reputable diving centres that cater to both beginners and experienced divers.

Embark on a voyage of discovery along the Turquoise Coast, where every coastal town, every ancient ruin, and every sailing adventure unfolds a story of Mediterranean magic. From the pristine beaches of Antalya to the sunken city of Kekova, the Turquoise Coast invites you to experience a blend of natural wonders and historical treasures—a tapestry woven with the colours of the sea and the echoes of civilizations that have shaped this coastal paradise.

Cappadocia: A Fairy Tale Landscape

In the heart of Central Anatolia, Turkey, lies a landscape that defies imagination—a realm of surreal rock formations, cave dwellings, and a skyline adorned with drifting hot air balloons. Cappadocia, often described as a fairy tale come to life, is a destination that transcends the ordinary. Join us on a journey through this otherworldly region, where every cave, every hoodoo, and every sunrise balloon ride tells a story of a land shaped by nature and myth.

Göreme: The Gateway to Cappadocia's Wonders

As you approach the region of Cappadocia, the town of Göreme emerges as the gateway to a fairy tale landscape. Nestled within a vast valley, Göreme is a charming town surrounded by surreal rock formations known as fairy chimneys. The unique geological features of Cappadocia are a result of volcanic activity that occurred millions of years ago, shaping the soft tuff rock into a whimsical landscape.

Begin your exploration in Göreme by visiting the Göreme Open-Air Museum, a UNESCO World Heritage Site. Wander through the ancient cave churches adorned with vibrant frescoes, each telling stories from the early Christian period. The Dark Church, with its exceptionally well-preserved frescoes, offers a glimpse into the artistic and religious history of the region.

Hot Air Balloon Magic: A Sunrise Adventure

One of the most iconic experiences in Cappadocia is the ethereal hot air balloon ride at sunrise. As the first light of dawn bathes the landscape in hues of pink and gold, the balloons ascend, transforming the sky into a canvas of dreams. Drifting silently over the fairy chimneys and valleys, you'll witness the true magic of Cappadocia from a perspective that is both enchanting and surreal.

The hot air balloon experience is not merely a ride; it's a journey into the heart of Cappadocia's fantastical terrain. Glide over the valleys of Love and Rose, named for the hues they take on during sunrise. Witness the sunrise casting its golden glow on the rock formations, creating a breath-taking panorama that seems straight out of a storybook. The fairy chimneys, ancient cave dwellings, and patchwork fields below become a living tapestry of Cappadocia's allure.

Ürgüp: Cave Dwellings and Vineyards

Venture to Ürgüp, a town surrounded by vineyards and apricot orchards, where the landscape seamlessly blends the ancient with the contemporary. Ürgüp is renowned for its cave hotels, carved into the soft rock, offering a unique and immersive experience. Stay in a cave room and awaken to the rustic charm of Cappadocian mornings, surrounded by the tranquillity of the rock-hewn architecture.

Explore the nearby Göreme Valley, where fairy chimneys and cave dwellings dot the landscape. Discover the ancient cave churches of St. Basil and St. Theodore, each revealing the intricate artistry of Cappadocia's early Christian period. In Ürgüp, you'll find yourself surrounded by a landscape that seems suspended in time, where every stone tells a tale of centuries gone by.

Love Valley: A Surreal Landscape

Embark on a journey to Love Valley, where the landscape takes on a surreal and romantic quality. The valley, named for its phallic-shaped fairy chimneys, invites visitors to explore its unique rock formations and meandering pathways. As you traverse the valley, the towering hoodoos create a dreamlike atmosphere, and the natural sculptures seem to whisper secrets of a bygone era.

Hike through the valley, allowing the whimsical shapes of the fairy chimneys to captivate your imagination. The contrast of the soft, white rock against the vivid blue sky creates a visual spectacle that is both awe-inspiring and surreal. Love Valley is not only a geological wonder but also a canvas for the imagination, where the boundaries between reality and fantasy blur.

Çavuşin: Ancient Cave Settlements

Journey to Çavuşin, an ancient settlement that showcases the evolution of cave dwelling architecture in Cappadocia. The town, perched on a hill overlooking the valley, is home to the Çavuşin Castle—a rock-cut structure that has witnessed centuries of history. Explore the narrow alleys and cave houses, each carved into the soft tuff rock, revealing the resilience of a community that adapted to the unique landscape.

Visit the Church of St. John the Baptist, a cavernous structure adorned with frescoes that narrate biblical stories. The church, dating back to the 5th century, offers a glimpse into the religious and artistic heritage of Cappadocia. From the heights of Çavuşin, the panoramic view of the surrounding valleys and fairy chimneys provides a captivating perspective of the region's geological wonders.

Paşabağ: Monks Valley and Mushroom Rocks

Delve into the whimsical landscape of Paşabağ, also known as Monks Valley, where the fairy chimneys take on peculiar shapes reminiscent of mushrooms. The valley, named for the hermit monks who once sought solitude in its unique formations, is a playground of nature's creativity. The mushroom-shaped rocks, with their slender stems and capped heads, evoke a sense of wonder and enchantment.

Explore the pathways that wind through the valley, marvelling at the intricacies of the rock formations. The erosion that shaped these geological wonders has created a natural sculpture garden, where each hoodoo stands as a testament to the sculpting hands of time. Paşabağ is a surreal destination that invites contemplation and exploration—a testament to the artistic prowess of nature.

Avanos: Pottery and the Red River

Visit Avanos, a town with a rich tradition of pottery making that dates back to the Hittite period. Nestled along the banks of the Red River (Kızılırmak), Avanos offers a serene setting for artisans to practice their craft. Take a stroll through the town's cobbled streets, lined with pottery workshops and galleries showcasing a diverse array of ceramic art.

Participate in a hands-on pottery workshop, where skilled artisans share their expertise and guide you in creating your own masterpiece. The distinctive red clay of Avanos, sourced from the banks of the Red River, has been used for centuries to craft pottery that reflects the region's artistic heritage. Avanos is not just a destination for acquiring unique ceramics; it's an opportunity to connect with the age-old craft that defines the spirit of Cappadocia.

Derinkuyu Underground City: A Subterranean Enigma

Unravel the mysteries of Cappadocia's subterranean world by exploring the Derinkuyu Underground City—a vast network of tunnels, chambers, and living spaces carved into the soft rock. Derinkuyu is one of several underground cities in the region, created by ancient inhabitants to escape invasions and provide shelter during times of peril.

Descend into the depths of Derinkuyu to discover a labyrinthine city that extends several levels below the surface. Explore living quarters, communal spaces, and even a chapel, all hewn from the rock. The ingenious ventilation and storage systems showcase the advanced engineering skills of the ancient residents. Derinkuyu is a testament to the resilience and resourcefulness of the people who called Cappadocia home.

Practical Tips for Exploring Cappadocia:

- Balloon Ride Reservations: Hot air balloon rides are a highlight of Cappadocia, and it's advisable to book in advance, especially during peak seasons. Consider opting for a sunrise flight to witness the magical dawn over the fairy chimneys.

- Comfortable Footwear: Many of Cappadocia's attractions involve walking on uneven terrain. Comfortable, sturdy footwear is recommended, especially if you plan to explore valleys, cave churches, and hiking trails.

- Weather Considerations: Cappadocia experiences distinct seasons. While the region is enchanting in every season, be mindful of weather conditions, especially if you plan to participate in outdoor activities like hiking.

- Cave Accommodations: Consider staying in a cave hotel for a truly immersive experience. Many hotels in Göreme, Ürgüp, and other towns offer cave rooms with modern amenities, allowing you to experience the charm of Cappadocian living.

Embark on a journey through the fairy tale landscape of Cappadocia, where every hoodoo, every cave dwelling, and every hot air balloon ride tells a story of a region shaped by nature's hand and steeped in myth and history. Whether exploring the ancient cave churches of Göreme or drifting over the surreal landscapes in a hot air balloon, Cappadocia invites you to step into a world where reality and fantasy dance in harmony—a landscape that transcends time and captures the imagination like no other.

Anatolian Adventures: Off the Beaten Path

Beyond the well-trodden tourist paths lies a tapestry of hidden gems, untold stories, and local experiences waiting to be discovered. Anatolia, a vast region in Turkey with a history as rich and diverse as its landscapes, beckons the intrepid traveller to venture off the beaten path. Join us on a journey through lesser-known corners of Anatolia, where ancient traditions, natural wonders, and warm hospitality create an authentic tapestry of discovery.

Amasya: A Riverside Gem

Nestled between the mountains and the Yesilırmak River, Amasya is a picturesque town that exudes charm and history. The city's skyline is adorned with Ottoman-era houses perched on the cliffs, creating a scene that feels suspended in time. Stroll along the riverside promenade, where the reflection of Amasya's historic structures dances on the calm waters.

Explore the Amasya Museum, housed in an old Ottoman mansion, to trace the region's history from prehistoric times to the present day. Visit the Hazeranlar Mansion, an exquisite example of Ottoman architecture, and the Tombs of the Kings, carved into the cliffs overlooking the city. Amasya is not only a destination for history enthusiasts but also a haven for those seeking the tranquillity of a riverside retreat.

Safranbolu: A Journey to the Ottoman Past

Step into the enchanting world of Safranbolu, a UNESCO World Heritage Site that preserves the charm of Ottoman architecture. The town, known for its well-preserved houses, cobbled streets, and traditional Turkish baths, invites visitors to embark on a journey back in time. Safranbolu earned its name from saffron, once a valuable spice traded along the historic Silk Road.

Wander through the Çarşı District, where the scent of spices lingers in the air, and explore the Cinci Han, an Ottoman-era caravanserai that speaks of the town's mercantile past. Visit the Safranbolu Museum, housed in a restored Ottoman mansion, to delve into the town's history. As the sun sets, Safranbolu's streets are bathed in a warm glow, transporting you to an era when caravans traversed these ancient routes.

Hattusa: Capital of the Hittites

Venture into the heart of Anatolia to discover the ancient city of Hattusa, the capital of the Hittite Empire. Located near modern-day Boğazkale, Hattusa is a UNESCO World Heritage Site that unveils the remnants of a civilization that flourished over 3,500 years ago. The city's imposing walls, once adorned with decorative gates and towers, provide a glimpse into the grandeur of Hittite architecture.

Explore the Great Temple, dedicated to the Hittite storm god, and the Yazılıkaya Open Air Sanctuary, featuring rock reliefs depicting Hittite deities. Walk along the city walls, where stone reliefs and inscriptions tell stories of Hittite kings and their achievements. Hattusa is a captivating destination for history enthusiasts, offering a window into a civilization that played a crucial role in the ancient world.

Eğirdir: Tranquility by the Lake

Discover the serenity of Eğirdir, a town nestled on the shores of Lake Eğirdir—a hidden gem in the heart of Anatolia. The lake, surrounded by mountains and olive groves, reflects the changing colours of the sky, creating a tranquil setting for relaxation and exploration. Eğirdir offers a welcome escape from the bustling city life, inviting visitors to savour the beauty of nature and the warmth of local hospitality.

Take a boat ride on Lake Eğirdir to explore the island of Yeşilada, home to a historic castle and the Church of St. Nicholas. Wander through the old town, where Ottoman-era houses and narrow streets transport you to a bygone era. The Eğirdir Citadel, perched on a hill overlooking the lake, provides panoramic views of the surrounding landscape. Eğirdir is a destination for those seeking tranquillity, where the rhythm of life is set by the gentle lapping of the lake against the shore.

Phrygian Valley: Land of Rock Cut Monuments

Embark on a journey through the Phrygian Valley, an ancient region adorned with rock-cut monuments, tombs, and temples. The Phrygians, an ancient Anatolian people, left their mark on the landscape in the form of intriguing rock formations and structures. Explore the Phrygian Road, a network of paths that connect the region's ancient sites and showcase the ingenuity of Phrygian engineering.

Visit the Midas Monument, named after the legendary King Midas, and the Gordion Archaeological Site, where the Phrygian capital once stood. Marvel at the rock-cut tombs of Yazılıkaya and the Phrygian Valley Open-Air Museum, featuring an array of carved facades and reliefs. The Phrygian Valley is a testament to the artistic and architectural achievements of an ancient civilization that thrived in the heart of Anatolia.

Divriği: The Grand Mosque and Hospital Complex

Step into the town of Divriği, home to one of the most exquisite examples of Islamic architecture—the Divriği Great Mosque and Hospital. This UNESCO World Heritage Site, built in the 13th century, is a masterpiece of Seljuk Turkish architecture. The complex, commissioned by the local ruler Emir Ahmet Shah and his wife Melike Turan, showcases intricate stonework, ornate decorations, and a harmonious blend of religious and medical functions.

Explore the prayer hall of the mosque, adorned with exquisite decorations and a mihrab (prayer niche) that exemplifies Islamic artistic traditions. Marvel at the intricately carved portal of the mosque and the adjacent hospital, a testament to the cultural and intellectual achievements of the Anatolian Seljuks. Divriği invites travellers to delve into the intersection of art, religion, and healthcare in medieval Anatolia.

Assos: A Seaside Retreat with Ancient Roots

Nestled on the Aegean coast, Assos is a seaside retreat with a history that traces back to ancient times. The city, founded by colonists from the island of Lesbos, offers a harmonious blend of natural beauty and archaeological wonders. Explore the ruins of the ancient city, where the Temple of Athena, the acropolis, and the theatre overlook the azure waters of the Aegean Sea.

Wander through the narrow streets of Behramkale, the charming village that has grown around the ancient site, and discover traditional Ottoman houses and local artisans. As the sun sets over the Aegean, dine in a seaside taverna and savour the flavours of Aegean cuisine. Assos is a destination where ancient history and contemporary tranquillity coexist, inviting visitors to unwind in the embrace of the sea.

Trabzon: Gateway to the Black Sea

Venture to Trabzon, a city that serves as the gateway to the lush landscapes of the Black Sea region. Surrounded by mountains and bordered by the Black Sea, Trabzon is a melting pot of cultures and histories. Explore the Hagia Sophia of Trabzon, a Byzantine church turned Ottoman mosque, adorned with frescoes that narrate the city's past.

Visit the Sumela Monastery, perched on a cliff overlooking a verdant valley. The monastery, founded in the 4th century, is a symbol of the region's rich religious and cultural heritage. Explore the bustling bazaars of Trabzon, where local traders offer an array of Black Sea specialties, including hazelnuts, tea, and regional delicacies. Trabzon is a destination where the echoes of empires and the rhythms of the Black Sea come together in a captivating blend.

Mount Ararat: The Legendary Peak

Embark on an adventure to Mount Ararat, the legendary peak that looms large in both geography and mythology. As the highest mountain in Turkey, Mount Ararat is a majestic sight that has captivated explorers and storytellers for centuries. The mountain is also believed to be the resting place of Noah's Ark, adding a layer of myth and mystery to its towering presence.

Embark on a trek to the base camp of Mount Ararat, where the landscapes transition from verdant meadows to rocky slopes. The ascent offers panoramic views of the surrounding region, including the vast plains of Eastern Anatolia. While reaching the summit requires mountaineering expertise, the journey to the base camp is a rewarding experience for those seeking adventure and a connection to the legendary narratives that surround Mount Ararat.

Practical Tips for Anatolian Adventures:

- Local Guides: In lesser-known regions, consider hiring local guides who can provide insights into the history, culture, and hidden gems of the area. Local guides often offer a more authentic and immersive experience.

- Language Considerations: While English is commonly spoken in tourist destinations, learning a few basic Turkish phrases can enhance your interactions and experiences, especially in more remote areas.

- Culinary Exploration: Anatolia is renowned for its diverse culinary traditions. Be adventurous and try local specialties in each region. From Black Sea cuisine in Trabzon to traditional Anatolian dishes in Safranbolu, each destination offers a unique culinary experience.

- Seasonal Considerations: Anatolia experiences diverse climates, from the Mediterranean in the south to the Black Sea in the north. Be mindful of seasonal variations, and plan your travels accordingly. Some regions, like Mount Ararat, may have limited accessibility during certain times of the year.

Embark on Anatolian adventures that lead you through the heart of Turkey's lesser-known regions. From the ancient mysteries of Hattusa to the tranquil shores of Lake Eğirdir, Anatolia invites you to step off the beaten path and uncover the hidden treasures that await in its diverse landscapes. In each destination, you'll encounter the warmth of local hospitality, the echoes of ancient civilizations, and the allure of a region that has been shaped by the hands of time and the spirit of exploration.

Turkish Hospitality: Staying with Locals

In the heart of Turkey, beyond the confines of standard accommodations, lies an opportunity to immerse oneself in the warmth of Turkish hospitality. From homestays in rural villages to guesthouses nestled in historic towns, experiencing Turkey through the eyes of locals is a journey into the heart and soul of the country. Join us on a guide through the art of staying with locals, where every shared meal, every heartfelt conversation, and every night under a hospitable roof becomes a chapter in your Turkish adventure.

Homestays in Cappadocia: Sharing Life in Fairy Chimneys

As you embark on your journey to Cappadocia, consider the allure of homestays in the midst of the fairy chimneys and cave dwellings. Numerous families in towns like Göreme and Ürgüp open their doors to travellers, providing an intimate glimpse into the daily life of the region. Picture waking up in a cave room carved into soft tuff rock, with the morning sun casting its gentle glow on the unique landscape outside your window.

Homestays in Cappadocia offer more than just a place to rest; they are a cultural exchange, a chance to partake in the daily routines of your hosts. Share a traditional Turkish breakfast with your host family, savouring olives, cheese, tomatoes, and freshly baked bread. Engage in conversations over çay (Turkish tea) in the courtyard, where the tales of Cappadocia come to life through the anecdotes shared by your hosts.

Explore the local markets alongside your host, picking fresh produce and spices that will later find their way into the dishes prepared for dinner. As evening descends, join in the preparation of a traditional meal, whether it's mantı (Turkish dumplings) or testi kebab (slow-cooked meat in a clay pot). The aromas wafting through the kitchen and the laughter shared around the dinner table create a tapestry of memories that transcend the ordinary.

Homestays in Cappadocia not only provide a comfortable and unique lodging experience but also foster connections that endure long after you've bid farewell to the fairy chimneys. The warmth of Turkish hospitality, embodied in the genuine smiles of your hosts and the shared moments of daily life, transforms a visit to Cappadocia into an immersive journey through the heart of Anatolia.

Village Retreats in the Aegean: Rustic Charms and Seaside Serenity

For a taste of village life along the Aegean coast, consider venturing into lesser-known rural retreats. Villages like Şirince in Izmir offer a tranquil escape, where the pace of life is set by the rhythms of nature and the embrace of rolling hills. Homestays in these villages provide an opportunity to unwind in rustic surroundings, savouring the simplicity of rural living.

Picture staying in a traditional stone house adorned with vibrant bougainvillea, surrounded by vineyards and orchards. Your hosts, often the owners of local vineyards or olive groves, invite you to explore the bounty of their land. Participate in the olive harvest, learning the art of pressing olive oil and tasting the rich flavours of the region. Wander through vineyards, where the sweet scent of ripening grapes fills the air, and join in the process of winemaking—a tradition passed down through generations.

Homestays in Aegean villages extend beyond the confines of accommodations; they are a portal into the heart of local traditions. Engage in the preparation of traditional dishes, such as börek (savoury pastry) or güveç (slow-cooked stew). Your hosts may share stories of their families, the history of the village, and the customs that define daily life. As the sun sets, gather on a terrace overlooking the Aegean

Sea, where the horizon meets the hues of a coastal sunset—a tranquil panorama that becomes a canvas for shared moments and newfound friendships.

Whether you choose a village retreat on the outskirts of Selçuk or a seaside homestay in the charming town of Alacati, the Aegean region unfolds its charms through the genuine hospitality of local hosts. Each homestay is an invitation to slow down, savour the simplicity of rural life, and forge connections that transcend the boundaries of language and culture.

Black Sea Guesthouses: Embracing Tradition and Tea

The Black Sea region, with its lush landscapes and vibrant culture, offers a unique setting for experiencing Turkish hospitality in guesthouses steeped in tradition. In towns like Safranbolu, perched on the edge of the Black Sea, guesthouses are often historic Ottoman-era homes that have been lovingly restored to offer modern comfort without sacrificing authenticity.

Immerse yourself in the charm of Safranbolu's Çarşı District, where cobblestone streets wind through a landscape adorned with Ottoman houses, each with its unique story. Guesthouses in Safranbolu often feature intricately carved wooden facades, antique furnishings, and panoramic views of the town's historic skyline. As you step through the doorway of a guesthouse, you step into a bygone era, where the echoes of Ottoman grandeur mingle with the warmth of Turkish hospitality.

Your hosts, often the custodians of these historic homes, share a passion for preserving the cultural heritage of Safranbolu. Engage in conversations with them over a cup of çay, learning about the history of the town and the traditions that have shaped its character. The guesthouse experience extends beyond the confines of your room; it's an invitation to explore the hidden corners of Safranbolu, where every alleyway, every mosque, and every marketplace reveals a facet of the town's rich heritage.

For a different perspective on the Black Sea, consider venturing into the lush hillsides surrounding the town of Rize. Guesthouses in this region often overlook tea plantations, where the verdant fields create a tapestry that stretches to the horizon. Join your hosts in the age-old tradition of tea cultivation, plucking tea leaves alongside local harvesters and witnessing the meticulous process that transforms leaves into the iconic Turkish çay.

Guesthouses in the Black Sea region not only provide a glimpse into the region's cultural heritage but also offer a serene retreat where the pace of life aligns with the gentle rustle of leaves and the aroma of freshly brewed tea. The authenticity of these guesthouses, paired with the genuine warmth of hosts, makes every stay a journey into the heart of Black Sea hospitality.

Countryside Escapes in Central Anatolia: A Tapestry of Fields and Fortresses

Escape to the heart of Central Anatolia, where the countryside unfolds as a patchwork of fields, fortresses, and timeless villages. Guesthouses in towns like Aksaray or Kırşehir are gateways to the vast landscapes that define the region. Here, you'll find the charm of rural life, where the day begins with the call of roosters and the aroma of freshly baked bread.

Guesthouses in Central Anatolia often reflect the architectural styles of the region, with stone exteriors, wooden details, and courtyards that invite relaxation. Your hosts, deeply connected to the agricultural rhythms of the countryside, may extend an invitation to explore their farms and orchards. Join in the planting or harvesting of crops, gaining insight into the traditions that sustain local livelihoods.

As evening descends, retreat to the guesthouse courtyard, where a feast of local delic

acies awaits. The cuisine of Central Anatolia, rich in flavours and rooted in tradition, becomes a centrepiece of your stay. Your hosts may introduce you to specialties such as manti (Turkish dumplings), etli ekmek (meat and dough dish), or börek, each dish a testament to the culinary heritage of the region.

Beyond the guesthouse, venture into the surrounding countryside, where ancient fortresses perch on hilltops and valleys reveal the traces of civilizations that once called Anatolia home. Explore the ancient city of Kültepe, known as Kanesh in antiquity, and discover the ruins of the Hittite civilization. Central Anatolia, with its guesthouses and rural retreats, is an invitation to uncover the layers of history that lie beneath the fertile soil and rolling hills.

Seaside Retreats on the Mediterranean: Sun, Sand, and Turkish Delights

For those seeking the allure of the Mediterranean, consider seaside retreats in towns like Kaş or Kalkan, where guesthouses offer a blend of coastal charm and Turkish hospitality. These guesthouses, often perched on hillsides overlooking the azure waters of the Mediterranean, provide a tranquil escape that combines the pleasures of sun-soaked beaches with the warmth of local welcome.

Imagine waking up to the gentle sound of waves and the scent of sea breeze drifting through your window. Guesthouses in the Mediterranean region are designed to capture the essence of coastal living, with whitewashed exteriors, terraces adorned with bougainvillea, and panoramic views of the turquoise waters. Your hosts, locals with a deep connection to the sea, may share stories of maritime traditions and the rhythms of life along the Mediterranean coast.

Guesthouses in the Mediterranean often feature traditional Turkish courtyards, where breakfast is a leisurely affair accompanied by views of the sea. Indulge in the flavours of the region, from freshly caught seafood to local olive oil and herbs. Your hosts may guide you to hidden coves and pristine beaches, where the Mediterranean invites you to bask in its sun-drenched embrace.

Beyond the beaches, venture into the ancient city of Patara, with its well-preserved ruins and expansive sandy shores. Explore the Lycian Way, a hiking trail that meanders along the coastline, revealing the natural beauty and historical wonders of the region. Seaside retreats on the Mediterranean are not just places to stay; they are gateways to a coastal lifestyle where every sunset, every stroll along the shore, and every shared moment with your hosts become a part of your Mediterranean tale.

Practical Tips for Staying with Locals:

- Cultural Sensitivity: Embrace local customs and traditions, showing respect for the cultural nuances of each region. Take cues from your hosts and learn about the customs that define daily life.

- Learn Basic Turkish Phrases: While many hosts in tourist destinations may speak English, learning a few basic Turkish phrases can enhance your interactions and demonstrate your appreciation for the local language.

- Flexible Itineraries: Staying with locals often leads to spontaneous experiences and unforeseen opportunities. Keep your itinerary flexible, allowing room for impromptu invitations and unexpected discoveries.

- Gifts of Appreciation: Consider bringing a small gift from your home country as a token of appreciation for your hosts. This gesture fosters goodwill and contributes to the cultural exchange.

- Participate in Local Life: Whether it's joining a harvest, helping with meal preparation, or engaging in traditional activities, actively participate in the daily life of your hosts. This not only enriches your experience but also fosters meaningful connections.

Embark on a journey through the heart of Turkey, where the true essence of the country unfolds in the warmth of Turkish hospitality. Homestays in Cappadocia, guesthouses along the Aegean, Black Sea retreats, countryside escapes in Central Anatolia, and seaside havens on the Mediterranean—all invite you to step into the homes and lives of locals. As you share meals, stories, and laughter with your hosts, you'll discover that the true magic of Turkey lies not only in its landscapes and landmarks but in the genuine warmth of its people.

Natural Wonders: National Parks and Landscapes

Turkey, a land where the echoes of ancient civilizations blend with the whispers of nature, boasts a diverse tapestry of natural wonders. From the cascading travertine terraces of Pamukkale to the surreal landscapes of Göreme, the country's national parks and landscapes invite travellers on a journey through geological marvels, pristine coastlines, and lush valleys. Join us on an exploration of Turkey's breath-taking natural beauty, where each destination is a chapter in the story of a land shaped by time and the hand of Mother Nature.

Pamukkale: The Cotton Castle's Cascading Beauty

Nestled in the southwest of Turkey, the town of Pamukkale is home to one of the country's most iconic natural wonders—the terraces of white travertine. Aptly named the "Cotton Castle," Pamukkale is a testament to the transformative power of mineral-rich thermal waters that have flowed over the landscape for millennia, leaving behind cascading pools of glistening white terraces.

As you approach Pamukkale, the sight of the terraces against the backdrop of the Denizli province's landscape is nothing short of mesmerizing. The terraces, created by the precipitation of calcium carbonate from the mineral-rich waters, resemble a series of tiered pools. Explore the terraces barefoot, allowing the warm waters to envelop your feet as you ascend from one level to another. The mineral-rich waters are not only a feast for the eyes but are also believed to have therapeutic properties.

Venture into Hierapolis, the ancient city perched atop Pamukkale, where the remnants of Roman baths, temples, and theatres add a historical dimension to the natural spectacle. The Roman Theatre, with its stunning views of the terraces below, offers a glimpse into the architectural prowess of the ancient city. The Cleopatra Pool, fed by thermal springs, invites visitors to swim amidst ancient ruins—an experience that seamlessly blends history and nature.

Göreme National Park: A Surreal Canvas of Fairy Chimneys

In the heart of Cappadocia, Göreme National Park unfolds as a surreal landscape dotted with fairy chimneys, cave dwellings, and otherworldly rock formations. Recognized as a UNESCO World Heritage Site, Göreme National Park is a testament to the whimsical hand of erosion that has shaped the soft tuff rock into a fantastical tableau.

As you explore Göreme, the iconic fairy chimneys—tall, slender rock formations topped with conical caps—become your companions. These unique structures, formed by the differential erosion of the rock, have served various purposes throughout history, from dwellings to churches. Wander through the Göreme Open-Air Museum, where ancient cave churches adorned with vibrant frescoes tell stories of the region's early Christian communities.

The landscape of Göreme is not only about geological wonders but also about the vibrant culture that has thrived amidst the rocky terrain. Engage with the locals, many of whom still inhabit cave dwellings passed down through generations. Consider staying in a cave hotel, where modern amenities merge seamlessly with the ancient charm of Cappadocian living.

One of the most enchanting experiences in Göreme is a hot air balloon ride at sunrise. Drift above the fairy chimneys and valleys as the first light of dawn bathes the landscape in hues of pink and gold. From the vantage point of a hot air balloon, Göreme unfolds as a living canvas where the boundaries between reality and fantasy blur, inviting you to witness the magic of Cappadocia from a celestial perspective.

Kaçkar Mountains National Park: Alpine Majesty in the Northeast

For those seeking the serenity of alpine landscapes, Kaçkar Mountains National Park in north eastern Turkey unfolds as a haven of pristine beauty. The Kaçkar Mountains, part of the Pontic Mountain Range, offer a dramatic backdrop of rugged peaks, glacial lakes, and verdant meadows—a setting that beckons nature enthusiasts, hikers, and those in search of untamed beauty.

Begin your exploration in the town of Ayder, a gateway to the Kaçkar Mountains, where traditional wooden houses and the sound of flowing streams set the stage for your mountain adventure. The Ayder Plateau, surrounded by mountains and forests, is a perfect base for exploring the national park. Consider staying in a local guesthouse, where the warmth of Turkish hospitality is complemented by the crisp mountain air.

Embark on hiking trails that lead to alpine lakes such as Karagöl and Samistal, where the reflection of snow-capped peaks creates a mirror-like effect on the tranquil waters. Traverse through valleys adorned with wildflowers, keeping an eye out for endemic plant species that thrive in the alpine environment. The Kaçkar Mountains are also a haven for birdwatchers, with species like the Caucasian black grouse and bearded vulture inhabiting the rugged terrain.

For the more adventurous, the ascent of Kaçkar's highest peak, Kaçkar Dağı, promises breath-taking panoramic views of the surrounding landscapes. The alpine majesty of Kaçkar Mountains National Park is a retreat into nature's grandeur—a destination where the rhythm of life is set by the rustling leaves, the call of mountain birds, and the timeless beauty of unspoiled wilderness.

Saklıkent Canyon: A Cool Oasis in the Turkish Riviera

In the midst of the scorching Turkish Riviera, Saklıkent Canyon emerges as a cool oasis—an unexpected marvel of nature carved into the Taurus Mountains. The canyon, meaning "Hidden City" in Turkish, stretches for 18 kilometres and features towering cliffs, rushing waters, and a refreshing stream that beckons visitors to escape the heat of the coastal plains.

Embark on a journey through the narrow gorge, where the canyon walls soar to heights of up to 300 meters. The cool waters of the fast-flowing stream accompany you as you navigate through the rocky passages. In some sections, the canyon narrows to a mere 2 meters, creating a sense of intimacy with the natural surroundings. Hike along the wooden walkways that crisscross the canyon, providing both safety and the opportunity to marvel at the geological wonders.

Saklıkent Canyon is not just about the thrill of exploration; it's also a place of relaxation and rejuvenation. Find a shaded spot along the stream to savour a picnic, or visit one of the riverside cafes serving traditional Turkish fare. The crisp mountain air, the sound of flowing water, and the towering canyon walls create an ambiance that contrasts with the sun-drenched beaches of the nearby Turkish Riviera.

For the more adventurous, Saklıkent offers the opportunity for canyoning—a thrilling activity that involves navigating the canyon's water-filled passages. With the guidance of experienced instructors, descend into the heart of Saklıkent, where the rush of water and the challenges of the terrain create an exhilarating adventure. Saklıkent Canyon is a hidden gem in the Turkish Riviera, inviting visitors to trade the sun-soaked beaches for the cool embrace of its rocky confines.

Antalya's Turquoise Coast: A Tapestry of Bays and Beaches

Along the south-western coast of Turkey, Antalya's Turquoise Coast unfolds as a tapestry of bays, beaches, and cliffs that kiss the crystal-clear waters of the Mediterranean. This region, known for its idyllic landscapes and ancient ruins, invites travellers to indulge in the pleasures of sun, sea, and the unparalleled beauty of the coastline.

Begin your exploration in Antalya, where the historic Old Town, known as Kaleiçi, beckons with its narrow cobblestone streets, Ottoman-era architecture, and vibrant bazaars. As you wander through the maze-like alleys, catch glimpses of the Mediterranean Sea beyond the city walls. Consider staying in a boutique hotel in Kaleiçi, where the charm of the past meets the comforts of modern hospitality.

Venture westward along the coast to discover the hidden gems of the Turquoise Coast. Explore the ancient city of Phaselis, nestled between pine forests and the sea, where the ruins of aqueducts, theatres, and harbours transport you to a bygone era. Relax on the pristine beaches of Cirali, where the natural beauty is complemented by the nesting grounds of loggerhead sea turtles.

Discover the hidden gem of Butterfly Valley, accessible only by boat, where a secluded bay is surrounded by steep cliffs covered in lush vegetation. As you anchor in the bay, the vibrant colours of butterflies dancing through the air create a magical ambiance. Hike through the valley, where the verdant landscape is a stark contrast to the azure waters of the Mediterranean.

Sail along the Turquoise Coast on a traditional wooden gulet, exploring the secluded coves and bays that dot the shoreline. The yacht journey becomes a leisurely exploration of the Lycian Way, a hiking trail that follows the coastline and reveals ancient ruins, panoramic viewpoints, and the coastal villages that have thrived for centuries.

For those seeking adventure, the cliffs of Olympos offer the thrill of rock climbing amidst stunning seaside vistas. The ruins of the ancient city of Olympos, scattered along the coast, add a historical dimension to the natural beauty of the region. The Turquoise Coast is not just a destination for sunbathing and swimming; it's a journey into the heart of the Mediterranean, where each bay and beach unveils a new facet of coastal splendour.

Lake Van: Eastern Anatolia's Sapphire Gem

In the heart of Eastern Anatolia, Lake Van stands as a sapphire gem—a vast expanse of freshwater surrounded by snow-capped mountains and historic landmarks. Turkey's largest lake, Van is not just a destination for nature lovers but also a cultural crossroads where history, mythology, and natural beauty converge.

Begin your exploration in the city of Van, where the historic Van Castle overlooks the lake and the surrounding landscapes. The castle, perched on a rocky outcrop, offers panoramic views of Lake Van and the Armenian Highlands beyond. Venture into the castle's inner chambers, where inscriptions and reliefs narrate the stories of ancient civilizations that once called this region home.

As you approach Lake Van, the vibrant hues of the water, ranging from deep blues to emerald greens, captivate the senses. Consider taking a ferry to Akdamar Island, where the Church of the Holy Cross stands as a medieval marvel. The church, adorned with intricate stone carvings, is a testament to the cultural diversity that has shaped the history of the region.

Practical Travel Tips: Navigating Language and Customs

Traveling to a new country is a thrilling adventure, and Turkey, with its rich history, diverse landscapes, and vibrant culture, offers a tapestry of experiences for every traveller. As you embark on your journey, understanding the local customs, navigating the language, and embracing cultural nuances will enhance your overall experience. Join us in this guide to practical travel tips that will help you seamlessly navigate Turkey's social landscape and connect with the heart of its unique traditions.

Understanding Turkish Etiquette: A Warm Welcome Awaits

Turkish people are renowned for their warm hospitality, and understanding a few key aspects of Turkish etiquette will help you engage with locals and make the most of your travels.

1. Greetings and Expressions of Respect:

- Merhaba: The most common way to say "hello" in Turkish.

- Teşekkür ederim: "Thank you." Politeness is highly valued in Turkish culture, and expressing gratitude is essential.

- Lütfen and rica ederim: "Please" and "You're welcome," respectively. Using polite phrases goes a long way in social interactions.

2. Shoes Off Indoors:

- It's customary to remove your shoes when entering someone's home. Some restaurants and traditional accommodations may also have this practice.

3. Modesty in Dress:

- While major cities like Istanbul are diverse and cosmopolitan, in more conservative areas, it's advisable to dress modestly, especially when visiting religious sites.

4. Respect for Elders:

- Turkish culture places high value on respect for elders. When entering a room, it's customary to greet the oldest person first.

5. Tea Culture:

- Tea (çay) is a ubiquitous part of Turkish social life. Accepting a cup of tea is a gesture of hospitality, and sharing tea with locals provides opportunities for meaningful conversations.

6. Bargaining in Bazaars:

- When shopping in markets (bazaars), bargaining is a common practice. Be polite but feel free to negotiate the price, especially in more traditional markets.

7. Turkish Delight and Sweets:

- If offered Turkish delight or other sweets, it's polite to accept and enjoy them. It's a gesture of hospitality and friendliness.

8. Dining Etiquette:

- It's customary to wait for the host or elder to start the meal. If invited to someone's home, bringing a small gift, such as sweets or flowers, is a thoughtful gesture.

Language Basics: Turkish for Travellers

While English is widely spoken in tourist areas, making an effort to learn a few basic Turkish phrases can greatly enrich your experience and show locals that you appreciate their language and culture.

THE ULTIMATE TRAVELLERS GUIDE TO TURKEY

1. Basics:

- Merhaba: Hello

- Teşekkür ederim: Thank you

- Evet: Yes

- Hayır: No

- Lütfen: Please

2. Greetings:

- Günaydın: Good morning

- İyi öğlenler: Good afternoon

- İyi akşamlar: Good evening

- İyi geceler: Good night

3. Numbers:

- Bir: One

- İki: Two

- Üç: Three

- On: Ten

4. Common Phrases:

- Nasılsınız?: How are you?

- Evet, lütfen: Yes, please

- Hayır, teşekkür ederim: No, thank you

- Benim adım [your name]: My name is [your name]

5. Courtesy Phrases:

- Hoş geldiniz: Welcome

- Güle güle: Goodbye (when someone is leaving)

- Kolay gelsin: Good luck (often said to someone working)

Transportation and Getting Around:

1. Public Transportation:

- Istanbulkart: In Istanbul, the Istanbulkart is a rechargeable card that can be used for buses, trams, metro, and ferries. It offers discounted fares compared to purchasing single tickets.

2. Taxis:

- Use Official Taxis: Opt for official taxis with meters. Ensure the driver starts the meter at the beginning of the journey.

3. Dolmuş:

- Shared minibusses known as dolmuş operate on set routes. They are a cost-effective and efficient way to travel short distances.

4. Intercity Travel:

- Buses: Intercity buses are a popular and comfortable way to travel between cities. Companies like Metro Turizm, Kamil Koç, and Ulusoy offer reliable services.

- Trains: The Turkish State Railways (TCDD) operates train services between major cities. The high-speed train network connects cities like Ankara, Istanbul, and Eskişehir.

5. Domestic Flights:

- Turkish Airlines: Turkey has a well-connected domestic flight network. Turkish Airlines is the major carrier, offering flights to various cities.

6. Driving:

- International Driving Permit: If you plan to rent a car, an international driving permit is recommended. Driving in major cities can be challenging, but it offers flexibility for exploring rural areas.

7. Currency and Payments:

- Turkish Lira (TRY): The official currency is the Turkish Lira. Credit cards are widely accepted in major cities, but it's advisable to have some cash, especially in more remote areas.

8. Health and Safety:

- Tap Water: In major cities, tap water is generally safe to drink. In more rural areas, consider drinking bottled water.

- Health Insurance: Ensure you have comprehensive travel insurance that covers medical emergencies.

Embracing Cultural Experiences:

1. Turkish Baths (Hamams):

- Modesty: When visiting a hamam, bring a swimsuit for women or swim trunks for men. It's customary to cover yourself with a towel while in shared spaces.

2. Tea Culture:

- Tea Houses: Visit local tea houses to experience Turkish tea culture. It's common to spend time chatting over tea, playing backgammon, or simply enjoying the view.

3. Turkish Cuisine:

- Street Food: Don't miss out on trying street food, such as simit (sesame-crusted bread rings) and döner kebab. Explore local markets for a taste of authentic Turkish flavours.

4. Festivals and Events:

- Timing: Check the calendar for local festivals and events. Participating in cultural celebrations offers unique insights into Turkish traditions.

5. Photography Etiquette:

- Ask Permission: When photographing people, especially in rural areas, ask for permission. Some locals may appreciate the gesture, while others may prefer not to be photographed.

6. Respect for Religious Sites:

- Dress Modestly: When visiting mosques or religious sites, dress modestly. Women may be required to cover their heads, and all visitors should remove their shoes.

7. Tipping:

- Service Charge: In restaurants, a service charge may be included in the bill. If not, a tip of around 5-10% is customary.

Weather Considerations:

1. Diverse Climates:

- Mediterranean: Hot summers, mild winters.

- Aegean: Similar to the Mediterranean with slightly cooler temperatures.

- Central Anatolia: Hot summers, cold winters.

- Black Sea: Mild, wet winters, and warm, humid summers.

- Eastern Anatolia: Harsh winters, warm summers.

2. Seasonal Activities:

- Beaches: Summer (June to August) is ideal for beach destinations.

- Skiing: Winter (December to February) is the ski season in places like Uludağ and Palandöken.

3. Ramadan:

- Observance: Ramadan is the Islamic holy month. Respectful behaviour during this time includes refraining from eating, drinking, and smoking in public spaces during daylight hours.

Staying Connected:

1. SIM Cards:

- Local Providers: Purchase a local SIM card for data and calls. Providers like Turkcell, Vodafone, and Türk Telekom offer prepaid packages.

2. Wi-Fi:

- Availability: Most hotels, restaurants, and cafes offer free Wi-Fi. However, in more remote areas, connectivity may be limited.

3. Emergency Services:

- Dial 112: For emergencies, dial 112 for medical assistance, police, or fire services.

4. Consulates:

- Know Location: Be aware of the location of your country's consulate in major cities. In case of emergencies, they can provide assistance.

5. Travel Apps:

- Google Maps: Download offline maps for areas with limited connectivity.

- Translator Apps: Apps like Google Translate can help bridge language barriers.

Conclusion:

Turkey, with its kaleidoscope of landscapes, rich history, and warm hospitality, invites travellers to immerse themselves in a cultural tapestry that spans continents and centuries. Navigating the language and customs of this diverse country enhances the journey, fostering connections with locals and unlocking the door to authentic experiences. As you explore the ancient wonders, vibrant markets, and natural landscapes of Turkey, let these practical travel tips be your companion, guiding you through the intricacies of this captivating destination. Whether you're sipping tea in Istanbul, marvelling at the terraces of Pamukkale, or traversing the fairy chimneys of Cappadocia, may your journey through Turkey be filled with discovery, warmth, and the joy of cultural exploration.

Festivals and Celebrations: Immersing in Local Traditions

Turkey, with its rich tapestry of cultural diversity and historical heritage, comes alive with a vibrant array of festivals and celebrations throughout the year. From ancient traditions to modern cultural events, each festival provides a unique window into the heart of Turkish culture. Join us on a journey through the calendar of events, where you can immerse yourself in the magic of local traditions, witness religious celebrations, and partake in the joyous festivities that define the soul of Turkey.

January

1. Mevlana Whirling Dervishes Festival - Konya:

- Date: 17th December – 17th January

- Description: The Mevlana Whirling Dervishes Festival in Konya is a mesmerizing celebration of the mystical Sufi tradition. Commemorating the death of the renowned Sufi poet Mevlana Rumi, the festival features whirling dervishes in a trance-like dance that symbolizes spiritual ascent. The Mevlana Museum, the final resting place of Rumi, becomes the focal point of this spiritual journey.

2. Camel Wrestling Festival - Selçuk:

- Date: Third Sunday in January

- Description: In the town of Selçuk, the Camel Wrestling Festival unfolds as a unique spectacle, blending tradition with entertainment. Camels adorned with colourful decorations engage in friendly bouts, showcasing strength and agility. The festival is a cultural experience, complete with traditional music, food stalls, and a vibrant atmosphere.

February

1. Kars Kafkasör Winter Festival - Kars:

- Date: February

- Description: The Kars Kafkasör Winter Festival celebrates the winter season in the snowy landscapes of Kars. The festival features traditional games, winter sports, and cultural performances. One of the highlights is the horse-drawn sleigh races, adding a touch of nostalgia to the wintry festivities.

2. Alanya International Culture and Art Days - Alanya:

- Date: February

- Description: The Alanya International Culture and Art Days showcase the diversity of artistic expressions, including music, dance, theatre, and visual arts. Held in various venues across Alanya, the festival promotes cultural exchange and appreciation for the arts, both traditional and contemporary.

March

1. Nevruz - Nationwide:

- Date: March 21st

- Description: Nevruz marks the arrival of spring and is celebrated across Turkey with vibrant festivities. Traditional dances, music performances, and the symbolic jumping over bonfires are integral parts of the celebrations. Join locals in welcoming the new season with joy and enthusiasm.

2. International Istanbul Film Festival - Istanbul:

- Date: March-April

- Description: The International Istanbul Film Festival is a prominent event in the Turkish cultural calendar. Showcasing a diverse selection of films from around the world, the festival attracts filmmakers, industry professionals, and cinema enthusiasts. Screenings, discussions, and awards ceremonies contribute to the dynamic atmosphere of this cinematic celebration.

April

1. Tulip Festival - Istanbul:

- Date: April

- Description: The Tulip Festival in Istanbul transforms the city into a colourful panorama of blooming tulips. Parks and public spaces are adorned with tulip displays in various hues, celebrating the flower's significance in Turkish culture. The festival also includes cultural events, concerts, and exhibitions.

2. International Izmir Short Film Festival - Izmir:

- Date: April

- Description: The International Izmir Short Film Festival is a platform for emerging filmmakers to showcase their creativity. The festival features short films from various genres, offering a glimpse into the world of independent cinema. Screenings, discussions, and workshops contribute to the festival's dynamic atmosphere.

May

1. International Bodrum Dance Festival - Bodrum:

- Date: May

- Description: The International Bodrum Dance Festival brings together dance enthusiasts, performers, and choreographers from around the world. The festival features a diverse range of dance styles, including traditional, contemporary, and experimental forms. Workshops, performances, and collaborative events contribute to the festival's lively atmosphere.

2. Hıdrellez - Nationwide:

- Date: May 5th-6th

- Description: Hıdrellez is a celebration that marks the arrival of spring. People gather in open spaces, make wishes, and participate in traditional activities such as tying ribbons to trees and dancing. The festival is a blend of ancient Anatolian traditions and folk beliefs.

June

1. Istanbul Music Festival - Istanbul:

- Date: June

- Description: The Istanbul Music Festival is a prestigious event that showcases classical music performances by international and Turkish musicians. Venues such as the Hagia Eirene Museum and the Harbiye Cemil Topuzlu Open-Air Theatre host concerts, recitals, and opera performances, creating a musical feast for enthusiasts.

2. Camel Wrestling Festival - Aydın:

- Date: June

- Description: The Camel Wrestling Festival in Aydın continues the tradition of camel wrestling, bringing together decorated camels in friendly competition. The festival is accompanied by traditional music, local food, and a festive atmosphere that attracts both locals and visitors.

July

1. Ephesus Festival - Selçuk:

- Date: July-August

- Description: The Ephesus Festival is a celebration of the arts held in the ancient city of Ephesus. The festival features classical music concerts, opera performances, and ballet productions in the historic venues of Ephesus, creating a unique fusion of cultural heritage and artistic expression.

2. International Istanbul Jazz Festival - Istanbul:

- Date: July

- Description: The International Istanbul Jazz Festival is a highlight for jazz enthusiasts, featuring performances by renowned international and Turkish jazz artists. Concerts take place in various venues across Istanbul, including historic sites, concert halls, and outdoor spaces.

August

1. Victory Day - Nationwide:

- Date: August 30th

- Description: Victory Day (Zafer Bayramı) commemorates the triumph of the Turkish forces in the Battle of Dumlupınar in 1922. Nationwide celebrations include parades, fireworks, and events paying tribute to the military and the founding leader, Mustafa Kemal Atatürk.

2. International Antalya Sand Sculpture Festival - Antalya:

- Date: August-September

- Description: The International Antalya Sand Sculpture Festival showcases incredible sand sculptures crafted by artists from around the world. The sculptures, often depicting mythical creatures, historical figures, and cultural symbols, create a temporary outdoor art gallery on the beaches of Antalya.

September

1. International Istanbul Biennial - Istanbul:

- Date: September-November

- Description: The International Istanbul Biennial is a major contemporary art event that takes place every two years. The biennial features a wide range of visual arts, including installations, performances, and exhibitions, and brings together artists and art enthusiasts from diverse backgrounds.

2. Cappadox - Cappadocia:

-

Date: September

- Description: Cappadox is a unique festival that combines music, contemporary art, and outdoor experiences in the captivating landscapes of Cappadocia. Attendees can enjoy live music performances, art installations, and outdoor activities, creating a multidimensional cultural experience.

October

1. International Istanbul Puppet Festival - Istanbul:

- Date: October

- Description: The International Istanbul Puppet Festival is a delightful celebration of puppetry, featuring performances by puppet artists from Turkey and around the world. The festival includes a diverse range of puppetry styles, from traditional to experimental, captivating audiences of all ages.

2. Ankara International Film Festival - Ankara:

- Date: October

- Description: The Ankara International Film Festival is a cinematic celebration that showcases a curated selection of international and Turkish films. The festival provides a platform for emerging filmmakers and contributes to the cultural vibrancy of the capital city.

November

1. Republic Day - Nationwide:

- Date: October 29th

- Description: Republic Day (Cumhuriyet Bayramı) celebrates the proclamation of the Turkish Republic in 1923. Nationwide celebrations include parades, concerts, and events honouring the founding leader, Mustafa Kemal Atatürk.

2. Istanbul International Short Film Festival - Istanbul:

- Date: November

- Description: The Istanbul International Short Film Festival is a platform for short films from both Turkish and international filmmakers. The festival showcases a diverse range of genres and provides a space for emerging talents to present their work to a wider audience.

December

1. Whirling Dervishes Ceremony - Konya:

- Date: Throughout the year, with special ceremonies during December

- Description: While the Mevlana Whirling Dervishes Festival in January is a major event, throughout the year, visitors to Konya can witness the mesmerizing Whirling Dervishes Ceremony. Held in the Mevlana Museum, the ceremony is a spiritual and visually captivating experience.

2. Istanbul Christmas Market - Istanbul:

- Date: December

- Description: The Istanbul Christmas Market brings festive cheer to the city, with stalls offering holiday treats, handmade crafts, and seasonal decorations. The market, often set in iconic locations such as Taksim Square, adds a touch of magic to the end of the year.

Unique Local Traditions

1. Oil Wrestling Festival - Edirne:

- Date: June

- Description: The Kirkpinar Oil Wrestling Festival in Edirne is one of the oldest wrestling festivals in the world, dating back to the 14th century. Wrestlers douse themselves in olive oil before engaging in traditional matches. The festival is a celebration of strength, skill, and camaraderie.

2. Hıdırellez Spring Festival - Edirne and Thrace region:

- Date: May 5th-6th

- Description: Hıdırellez Spring Festival is celebrated with various rituals in different regions. In Edirne and the Thrace region, people make wishes, tie ribbons to trees, and participate in activities symbolizing the renewal of nature. Traditional music and dance add to the festive atmosphere.

3. Kırkpınar Oil Wrestling Festival - Edirne:

- Date: June

- Description: The Kırkpınar Oil Wrestling Festival in Edirne is one of the oldest wrestling festivals in the world, dating back to the 14th century. Wrestlers douse themselves in olive oil before engaging in traditional matches. The festival is a celebration of strength, skill, and camaraderie.

4. Camel Wrestling Festival - Various Locations:

- Date: Various months

- Description: Camel wrestling festivals take place in various locations, including Aydın and Selçuk. The festivals showcase decorated camels engaging in friendly competitions, accompanied by traditional music, food, and a festive atmosphere.

5. Efe Festival - Selçuk:

- Date: May

- Description: The Efe Festival in Selçuk celebrates the traditional warriors known as Efe, who played a significant role in local history. The festival includes parades, performances, and competitions that pay homage to this cultural heritage.

6. Troya Festival - Çanakkale:

- Date: June

- Description: The Troya Festival in Çanakkale celebrates the historical significance of the ancient city of Troy. The festival includes reenactments, performances, and cultural events that bring the epic tales of Troy to life.

7. Camel Wrestling Festival - Selçuk:

- Date: January

- Description: The Camel Wrestling Festival in Selçuk is a unique celebration that blends tradition with entertainment. Adorned camels engage in friendly wrestling matches, creating a festive atmosphere complete with traditional music, food stalls, and cultural activities.

8. St. Nicholas Day - Demre:

- Date: December 6th

- Description: St. Nicholas Day in Demre, the birthplace of St. Nicholas (Santa Claus), is celebrated with religious ceremonies and festive events. Pilgrims and visitors gather to honour the legacy of St. Nicholas, and the town comes alive with music, processions, and cultural activities.

Tips for Festival-Goers:

1. Plan Ahead:

- Research the dates and locations of festivals you wish to attend. Plan your itinerary to include these cultural celebrations.

2. Cultural Sensitivity:

- Respect local customs and traditions during festivals. Be aware of any specific dress codes or rituals.

3. Local Cuisine:

- Explore local cuisine at festival stalls. Festivals often feature traditional dishes and street food unique to the region.

4. Tickets and Accommodations:

- For popular festivals, purchase tickets in advance. Book accommodations early, especially in smaller towns or during peak festival times.

5. Learn Basic Phrases:

- While many festival organizers and attendees may speak English, learning a few basic phrases in Turkish can enhance your interactions and show appreciation for the local language.

6. Participate in Activities:

- Immerse yourself in the festival atmosphere by participating in cultural activities, dances, and rituals. Engage with locals to truly experience the spirit of the event.

7. Capture the Moments:

- Festivals are vibrant and visually stunning. Capture the moments with your camera, but also take the time to be fully present and enjoy the experience.

8. Be Open-Minded:

- Embrace the unexpected. Festivals may present unique cultural practices or performances that differ from your own experiences. Approach them with an open mind and a willingness to learn.

From the mystical Whirling Dervishes ceremonies to the lively Camel Wrestling Festivals, Turkey's calendar is filled with events that reflect the diversity and richness of its cultural heritage. Whether you find yourself dancing in the streets during Nevruz or marvelling at sand sculptures in Antalya, each festival offers a glimpse into the soul of Turkey. As you traverse the country, let the rhythms of traditional music, the colours of festive decorations, and the warmth of local hospitality guide you through an unforgettable journey of celebration.

Adventure Seeker's Paradise: Outdoor Activities in Turkey

Turkey, with its diverse landscapes, ancient ruins, and rich cultural tapestry, is not only a treasure trove for history enthusiasts but also a haven for adventure seekers. From the rugged mountains of the Eastern Anatolia region to the azure waters of the Mediterranean, the country offers a plethora of outdoor activities that promise an adrenaline rush and a connection with nature like no other. Join us on a journey through the Adventure Seeker's Paradise, where we explore hiking trails, soar above surreal landscapes in hot air balloons, dive into the depths of the Mediterranean, and embark on thrilling experiences that will etch unforgettable memories into the heart of every adventurer.

Hiking Trails: Exploring Turkey on Foot

1. Lycian Way: A Coastal Odyssey

The Lycian Way, stretching along the south-western coast of Turkey, is a hiking trail that weaves through ancient ruins, remote villages, and pristine beaches. This long-distance trail, over 500 kilometres in length, offers a diverse range of landscapes, from pine-clad mountains to turquoise bays.

Begin your Lycian Way adventure in Ölüdeniz, a famous beach resort. The trail takes you through the ghost town of Kayaköy, once a bustling Greek village, and ascends to the summit of Mount Babadağ for breath-taking panoramic views. As you trek along the coast, encounter ancient Lycian tombs and amphitheatres, such as those in Patara and Myra.

The trail continues through the charming village of Kaş, known for its vibrant market and laid-back atmosphere. Traverse cliff sides and descend into hidden coves, where the crystal-clear waters of the Mediterranean beckon. The Lycian Way concludes in the town of Demre, home to the ancient city of Myra and the Church of St. Nicholas.

2. Cappadocia: Fairy Chimneys and Hidden Valleys

Cappadocia, with its otherworldly landscapes and cave dwellings, is not only a cultural wonder but also a paradise for hikers. Explore the unique rock formations, known as fairy chimneys, and meander through hidden valleys that unveil a geological spectacle.

Begin your Cappadocian adventure in Göreme, the heart of the region. Hike through the Love Valley, where phallic-shaped fairy chimneys rise from the ground, creating a surreal landscape. Explore the Red Valley, adorned with vibrant hues during sunset, and witness the kaleidoscope of colours reflecting off the rock formations.

For a more challenging hike, venture into the Rose Valley, named for the pinkish hue that bathes the landscape during sunrise and sunset. Follow the trails that lead to ancient cave churches, such as the Church of St. John the Baptist, adorned with well-preserved frescoes.

The White Valley, with its lunar-like terrain, offers a contrast to the red and rose hues of its neighbouring valleys. Hike through this surreal landscape and ascend to viewpoints that provide panoramic vistas of Cappadocia's captivating beauty.

3. Mount Ararat: Conquering Turkey's Tallest Peak

For seasoned mountaineers seeking a challenging ascent, Mount Ararat beckons with its snow-capped peak and storied history. As Turkey's highest mountain, Mount Ararat rises majestically near the border with Iran. The climb to the summit is not for the faint of heart, but the rewards include unparalleled views and a sense of accomplishment.

The ascent typically begins from the town of Doğubayazıt. The climb is a multi-day endeavour, involving traversing rocky terrain, crossing glaciers, and navigating challenging weather conditions. The reward for the effort is reaching the summit, where, on a clear day, the landscapes of eastern Turkey and beyond unfold in a breath-taking panorama.

Reaching an elevation of 5,137 meters (16,854 feet), Mount Ararat is a dormant volcano surrounded by myths and legends, including its association with the biblical story of Noah's Ark. As you stand on the summit, surrounded by the vastness of the Turkish landscape, you'll understand why this adventure is a coveted experience for mountaineers around the world.

Hot Air Ballooning: Soaring Over Surreal Landscapes

1. Cappadocia: A Sky borne Odyssey

Cappadocia's surreal landscapes are not just meant to be explored on foot—they are meant to be seen from the sky. Hot air ballooning over Cappadocia is a quintessential adventure that offers a bird's-eye view of the fairy chimneys, cave dwellings, and patchwork fields below.

As dawn breaks over the horizon, hot air balloons ascend into the sky, creating a mesmerizing spectacle against the backdrop of Cappadocia's unique rock formations. The experience is not only a visual feast but also a serene journey as you drift silently over valleys, vineyards, and ancient villages.

Opt for a sunrise hot air balloon ride to witness the first light of day illuminating the surreal landscape. The gentle breeze carries you over the valleys of Göreme and Love, providing a panoramic perspective of the geological wonders below. The experience is heightened as the rising sun bathes the fairy chimneys in golden hues, creating a dreamscape that feels straight out of a fairy-tale.

2. Pamukkale: Ballooning Over the Cotton Castle

Pamukkale, known as the "Cotton Castle" for its terraces of white travertine, offers a unique hot air ballooning experience that combines natural beauty with historical marvels. As you ascend into the sky, the terraces of Pamukkale unfold below, creating a surreal canvas of white pools and cascading mineral-rich waters.

The hot air balloon ride over Pamukkale allows you to witness the geological wonders from a different perspective. Drift over the ancient ruins of Hierapolis, where Roman theatres and temples stand in silent testimony to the city's rich history. The experience is not only a visual feast but also an opportunity to capture the stunning contrast between the white travertine terraces and the lush greenery of the surrounding landscape.

Balloon rides in Pamukkale are typically scheduled during the early morning or late afternoon when the sunlight casts a warm glow on the terraces. The tranquillity of the experience, coupled with the awe-inspiring views, makes hot air ballooning over Pamukkale an adventure that combines history, nature, and the thrill of floating above a UNESCO World Heritage Site.

Scuba Diving: Exploring the Depths of the Mediterranean

1. Kas: Underwater Wonders of the Turkish Riviera

The Turkish Riviera, with its crystal-clear waters and vibrant marine life, beckons scuba diving enthusiasts to explore the underwater wonders of the Mediterranean. Kas, a charming coastal town, serves as a gateway to a diverse range of dive sites, offering experiences for both novice and experienced divers.

Dive into the Blue Cave, a submerged cavern illuminated by rays of sunlight that filter through the water,

Creating an ethereal underwater world. Explore the ancient shipwrecks that lie on the seabed, offering a glimpse into maritime history. The underwater landscapes of Kas are adorned with colourful coral reefs, teeming with schools of fish, octopuses, and sea turtles.

The diverse underwater topography includes walls, canyons, and caverns, providing a variety of dive experiences. From shallow dives suitable for beginners to deep dives for advanced divers, Kas offers a spectrum of underwater adventures. Dive sites such as the Incebogaz Cave and the Canyon showcase the rich biodiversity of the Mediterranean, making each descent into the depths a journey of discovery.

2. Bodrum: Exploring the Aegean's Underwater Treasures

Bodrum, a vibrant coastal town on the Aegean Sea, is not only known for its historical sites but also for its captivating underwater landscapes. The Bodrum Peninsula offers a range of dive sites that cater to all levels of expertise, ensuring that both beginners and seasoned divers can explore the depths of the Aegean.

The clear waters of the Aegean reveal a world of marine life and underwater formations. Dive sites such as the Aquarium and the Cave of Ince Burun feature colourful coral reefs, schools of fish, and the occasional encounter with larger marine species such as groupers and barracudas. The underwater topography includes rocky formations, swim-throughs, and underwater caves, adding an element of adventure to every dive.

Bodrum's dive centres provide certification courses for those new to scuba diving, allowing them to explore the vibrant underwater world under the guidance of experienced instructors. For certified divers, the opportunity to embark on boat dives to remote sites, such as the Black

Island and the Rabbit Island, adds an extra dimension to the scuba diving experience in Bodrum.

Rock Climbing: Scaling Turkey's Vertical Frontiers

1. Geyikbayırı: Climbing in Antalya's Limestone Wonderland

Geyikbayırı, located just a short drive from Antalya, is a rock climber's paradise, offering limestone cliffs and challenging routes in a stunning natural setting. The climbing area is surrounded by pine forests and boasts a wide range of routes suitable for climbers of all levels, from beginners to advanced.

The white limestone cliffs of Geyikbayırı provide a unique climbing experience, with routes that vary in difficulty and style. Climbers can ascend vertical faces, tackle overhangs, and navigate technical slabs, all while enjoying panoramic views of the surrounding landscape. The climbing season in Geyikbayırı extends from autumn to spring, making it an ideal destination for those seeking outdoor adventure during the cooler months.

The climbing community in Geyikbayırı is vibrant and inclusive, with climbers from around the world converging to share experiences and tackle the diverse range of routes. The area's accessibility from Antalya and the abundance of climbing options make Geyikbayırı a must-visit destination for rock climbing enthusiasts.

2. Aladağlar National Park: Vertical Wilderness in Central Anatolia

Aladağlar National Park, located in the Taurus Mountains of Central Anatolia, is a haven for rock climbers seeking vertical challenges amidst a pristine wilderness. The park is renowned for its granite rock formations, offering a diverse array of climbing opportunities, from single-pitch routes to multi-pitch adventures.

The climbing areas within Aladağlar encompass a variety of landscapes, including forests, alpine meadows, and rugged peaks. The rock quality is excellent, with routes that cater to climbers with varying skill levels. As you ascend the granite walls, you'll be treated to panoramic views of the surrounding mountains and valleys.

The climbing season in Aladağlar spans from spring to autumn, with the cooler months providing optimal conditions for vertical pursuits. Camping facilities within the national park offer climbers the opportunity to immerse themselves in the natural beauty of the Taurus Mountains while enjoying the camaraderie of the climbing community.

White-Water Rafting: Navigating Turkey's Rapids

1. Köprülü Canyon: Rapids and Ruins

Köprülü Canyon, located in the Antalya region, not only offers white-water rafting adventures but also combines the thrill of navigating rapids with the allure of ancient ruins. The Köprüçay River, flowing through the canyon, provides the perfect setting for adrenaline-pumping rafting excursions.

The rafting route in Köprülü Canyon takes you through a series of exciting rapids, surrounded by lush greenery and towering cliffs. As you paddle through the foaming waters, the ancient Roman Bridge (Oluk Bridge) comes into view, adding a historical dimension to the adventure. The bridge, dating back to the 2nd century, spans the river and serves as a scenic backdrop for rafters.

The rafting experience in Köprülü Canyon is suitable for both beginners and experienced rafters, with various sections offering different levels of difficulty. The adventure culminates with a sense of accomplishment and the opportunity to explore the nearby ancient city of Selge, where remnants of amphitheatres and temples await.

2. Dalaman River: Rapids and Wilderness

The Dalaman River, flowing through the picturesque Dalaman Valley, provides a white-water rafting experience surrounded by unspoiled wilderness. The river's rapids cater to a range of skill levels, making it an ideal destination for families, friends, and adventure seekers looking to navigate the rushing waters.

The rafting journey on the Dalaman River takes you through a landscape of pine forests, rocky gorges, and scenic valleys. The rapids offer an exhilarating challenge, and the calm stretches provide opportunities to soak in the natural beauty of the surroundings. The clear waters of the river, coupled with the backdrop of the Taurus Mountains, create a serene yet dynamic setting for the adventure.

Dalaman's white-water rafting trips are often complemented by opportunities for swimming, cliff jumping, and riverside picnics. The adventure allows participants to connect with nature while experiencing the thrill of navigating rapids in the heart of south-western Turkey.

Paragliding: Soaring High Above the Landscapes

1. Ölüdeniz: Gliding Over the Blue Lagoon

Ölüdeniz, with its iconic Blue Lagoon and stunning coastal landscapes, is not just a beach destination—it's also a premier paragliding location. The tandem paragliding experience in Ölüdeniz offers a unique perspective of the turquoise waters, sandy beaches, and rugged cliffs that define this picturesque corner of south-western Turkey.

The paragliding adventure typically begins from the summit of Mount Babadağ, a towering peak that overlooks Ölüdeniz. As you launch into the sky, the Blue Lagoon unfolds below, creating a mesmerizing panorama. The tandem flight allows participants to enjoy the experience with a certified pilot, ensuring both safety and the freedom to savour the beauty of the landscapes.

Soar above the coastline, feeling the rush of wind as you glide gracefully through the air. The flight path takes you over the Blue Lagoon, providing a bird's-eye view of the pristine waters and the sandy beaches that attract sun seekers from around the world. The descent concludes with a gentle landing on the beach, leaving participants with memories of an exhilarating adventure.

Shopping in Turkey: Souvenirs and Beyond

Turkey, a country that straddles the crossroads of Europe and Asia, boasts a rich tapestry of culture, history, and craftsmanship. As you traverse its vibrant cities and historic towns, the allure of Turkish markets, bazaars, and traditional crafts beckons. Embark on a journey through the sensory delights of shopping in Turkey, where every market stall tells a story, and every handcrafted item carries the imprint of centuries-old traditions.

Introduction: The Art of Turkish Shopping

To shop in Turkey is to engage in an ancient tradition, a dance of barter and discovery that has echoed through the centuries. From the bustling bazaars of Istanbul to the quaint artisan workshops in Cappadocia, the country offers a kaleidoscope of shopping experiences. Whether you seek exquisite textiles, intricate ceramics, or the perfect spice blend, Turkish markets are treasure troves waiting to be explored. Join us as we unravel the secrets of shopping in Turkey, where every purchase is a piece of the country's rich heritage.

1. The Grand Bazaar - Istanbul's Labyrinth of Treasures

The heartbeat of Istanbul's shopping scene, the Grand Bazaar stands as one of the world's oldest and largest covered markets. A kaleidoscope of colours and scents, this labyrinthine market is a microcosm of Turkish craftsmanship and trade. As you step into its bustling lanes, prepare to be enveloped by the harmonious chaos of vendors hawking everything from spices to gold.

Navigating the Grand Bazaar:

The Grand Bazaar, or Kapalıçarşı in Turkish, is a vast complex of covered streets and alleys, each dedicated to a specific type of merchandise. Here's your guide to navigating this historic marketplace:

Jewellery and Precious Metals: Start your journey in the Bedesten, the oldest part of the bazaar, where jewellers and goldsmiths showcase their intricate designs. From Ottoman-style rings to modern creations, the range is as diverse as Turkey's history.

Carpets and Textiles: Meander through the Cevahir Bedesten, where a sea of vibrant Turkish carpets awaits. Marvel at the artistry of hand-woven kilims and sumptuous silk carpets. Don't miss the chance to haggle; it's an integral part of the experience.

Spices and Sweets: Follow the aroma of exotic spices to the Egyptian Bazaar, also known as the Spice Bazaar, an extension of the Grand Bazaar. Sample Turkish delight, stock up on saffron and sumac, and lose yourself in the world of sensory delights.

Ceramics and Tiles: Explore the maze of shops offering dazzling Turkish ceramics, from intricate tiles to hand-painted plates. The patterns tell stories of Ottoman motifs and traditional Turkish designs.

Leather Goods: If leather is on your list, head to the Leather Bedesten for a selection of high-quality goods, from bags to jackets. Turkish leather is renowned for its craftsmanship, and the bazaar offers an array of options to choose from.

Navigational Tips:

- Get Lost Deliberately: The joy of the Grand Bazaar lies in getting lost and discovering hidden gems. Don't be afraid to wander off the main paths.

- Bargaining is expected: Embrace the art of bargaining, but do so with respect and a smile. It's part of the cultural exchange.

2. The Spice Bazaar - A Culinary Wonderland in Istanbul

Adjacent to the Galata Bridge, the Spice Bazaar, also known as the Egyptian Bazaar, is a sensory feast that immerses you in the world of Turkish flavours. As you step inside, the air becomes infused with the heady scents of spices, teas, and exotic sweets. This bustling market is not just a shopping destination; it's a culinary journey through the heart of Turkish cuisine.

Exploring the Spice Bazaar:

Spices and Herbs: The Spice Bazaar is a spice connoisseur's dream. From crimson saffron to earthy cumin, the vibrant stalls showcase the diversity of Turkish spices. Engage with the vendors, who are often passionate about their products, and learn about the unique blends used in Turkish cooking.

Turkish delight and Sweets: Indulge your sweet tooth with a visit to the stalls laden with Turkish delight (lokum), baklava, and other traditional sweets. The colourful displays are a treat for the eyes, and sampling these delights is an essential part of the experience.

Tea and Coffee: Turkish tea and coffee are integral to the nation's culture. Explore stalls offering a variety of teas, including apple tea, sage tea, and the ubiquitous Turkish black tea. Don't forget to pick up a traditional Turkish coffee set for an authentic brewing experience.

Dried Fruits and Nuts: From apricots to figs, the Spice Bazaar is a paradise for dried fruit enthusiasts. The stalls also feature an assortment of nuts, offering a healthy and delicious snack.

Natural Remedies: Delve into the world of herbal remedies as you explore stalls offering a range of medicinal herbs and traditional Turkish remedies. The vendors often share insights into the healing properties of the herbs they sell.

Navigational Tips:

- Sample Freely: Many vendors offer samples of their products. Take advantage of this and taste a variety of spices, sweets, and teas before making your purchases.

- Engage with Locals: Strike up conversations with the vendors. They often have fascinating stories about the origin of their products and can provide valuable insights into Turkish culinary traditions.

3. Çarşı: Alaçatı's Bohemian Shopping Haven

Alaçatı, a charming town on the Çeşme Peninsula, is renowned for its cobblestone streets, historic stone houses, and vibrant markets. The heart of shopping in Alaçatı is Çarşı, a bohemian haven where traditional craftsmanship meets contemporary design. From chic boutiques to quaint cafes, Çarşı invites you to explore its eclectic offerings.

Discovering Çarşı:

Boutique Fashion: Alaçatı has earned a reputation as a fashion-forward destination, and Çarşı reflects this with its array of boutique stores. From locally designed clothing to handmade accessories, you'll find unique pieces that capture the essence of Turkish style.

Artisanal Crafts: Wander through Çarşı's narrow lanes to discover artisanal workshops and boutiques showcasing handmade crafts. Ceramics, jewellery, and leather goods crafted by local artisans offer a blend of tradition and modernity.

Antiques and Vintage Finds: Antique enthusiasts will appreciate the curated selection of vintage shops in Çarşı. Explore hidden corners to uncover treasures that span eras, from Ottoman artefacts to mid-century modern pieces.

Cafes and Restaurants: Çarşı isn't just about shopping; it's a lifestyle experience. Pause for a leisurely coffee or indulge in a delicious meal at one of the charming cafes or restaurants that dot the streets. The ambiance is as delightful as the cuisine.

Navigational Tips:

- Explore Side Streets: While the main thoroughfare of Çarşı is bustling, don't hesitate to venture into the side streets. Many hidden gems await those who take the time to explore.

4. Eminönü and the Egyptian Bazaar: A Culinary Odyssey in Istanbul

Eminönü, located on the European side of Istanbul, is a district that bridges the old and the new. Here, the iconic Galata Bridge connects the historic heart of the city with the vibrant neighbourhoods beyond. Eminönü is not only a hub of transportation but also a culinary paradise where the aromas of street food blend with the sights and sounds of daily life.

Savouring Eminönü:

Balık Ekmek by the Galata Bridge: Begin your culinary adventure with a visit to the Galata Bridge, where the tantalizing scent of grilled fish beckons. Balık Ekmek, a Turkish fish sandwich, is a beloved street food. Watch as vendors skilfully grill the catch of the day and serve it in a fresh bread roll with salad and a squeeze of lemon.

Spice Up Your Senses at the Egyptian Bazaar: Adjacent to Eminönü, the Spice Bazaar (Misir Çarsisi), also known as the Egyptian Bazaar, is a haven for food enthusiasts. Explore stalls brimming with spices, dried fruits, nuts, and Turkish sweets. Don't miss the chance to sample olives of various varieties, each with its unique flavour profile.

Baklava at Güllüoğlu: A short stroll from the Spice Bazaar leads you to Güllüoğlu, a renowned pastry shop that has perfected the art of baklava. Indulge in layers of flaky pastry, nuts, and honey as you savour this quintessential Turkish dessert. The shop offers various baklava types, each a testament to centuries-old recipes.

Traditional Turkish delight at Hafız Mustafa 1864: For a sweet journey through Turkish delights, visit Hafız Mustafa 1864, a historic confectionery located near the Spice Bazaar. Established in 1864, the shop is celebrated for its traditional Turkish delight (lokum) in an array of flavours, including rose, pomegranate, and mint.

Navigational Tips:

- Join the Locals: The eateries around Eminönü are frequented by locals. Follow their lead to discover hidden gems that may not be in your guidebook.

- Plan for Crowds: Eminönü is a bustling district, especially during peak hours. Plan your visit with some flexibility to navigate the crowds.

5. The Arasta Bazaar - Hidden Gem by the Blue Mosque

Tucked away behind the Blue Mosque in Istanbul, the Arasta Bazaar is a hidden gem waiting to be discovered. This quaint market offers a more relaxed shopping experience compared to the Grand Bazaar, making it an ideal destination for those seeking authentic Turkish handicrafts without the hustle and bustle.

Exploring the Arasta Bazaar:

Turkish Carpets and Kilims: The Arasta Bazaar is known for its collection of Turkish carpets and kilims. The intricate designs and vibrant colours make these textiles unique, and the shopkeepers often share the stories behind each piece.

Handmade Ceramics: Delve into shops that showcase handmade Turkish ceramics, including plates, bowls, and tiles. The traditional blue-and-white patterns evoke the timeless beauty of Turkish pottery.

Antique and Vintage Finds: Antique enthusiasts will appreciate the curated selection of vintage shops in the Arasta Bazaar. Explore hidden corners to uncover treasures that span eras, from Ottoman artefacts to mid-century modern pieces.

Jewellery and Accessories: The bazaar features boutiques offering exquisite Turkish jewellery and accessories. From Ottoman-inspired designs to contemporary pieces, you'll find a range of options to suit every style.

Navigational Tips:

- Explore at a Leisurely Pace: The Arasta Bazaar is smaller than the Grand Bazaar, allowing you to explore at a more leisurely pace. Take the time to appreciate the craftsmanship and engage with the artisans.

- Combine with Mosque Visit: Since the Arasta Bazaar is situated near the Blue Mosque, consider combining your visit with a tour of this iconic landmark.

6. Çukurcuma: Istanbul's Antique District

For those enchanted by the allure of vintage treasures and timeless artefacts, Çukurcuma in Istanbul beckons with its cobblestone streets and a wealth of antique shops. Nestled in the Beyoğlu district, this charming neighbourhood is a haven for antique enthusiasts, collectors, and those seeking unique pieces that tell stories of a bygone era.

Exploring Çukurcuma:

Antique Shops Galore: Çukurcuma is renowned for its concentration of antique shops, each offering a curated selection of items that span centuries. From intricately carved furniture to vintage textiles, the shops invite you to step into a world where craftsmanship and history converge.

Art Galleries and Design Boutiques: Beyond antiques, Çukurcuma is home to art galleries and design boutiques that showcase the work of contemporary Turkish artists. The juxtaposition of old and new creates a dynamic atmosphere that reflects Istanbul's vibrant cultural scene.

Coffee and Bookshops: As you weave through the streets of Çukurcuma, take a moment to savour a cup of Turkish coffee in one of the charming cafes. Many bookshops in the area offer a selection of rare books and vintage editions, adding to the neighbourhood's intellectual charm.

Hidden Courtyards and Galleries: Çukurcuma is a neighborhood of surprises, with hidden courtyards and galleries waiting to be discovered. Wander off the main streets to explore these tucked-away spaces, where you may stumble upon art installations, exhibitions, or even live performances.

Navigational Tips:

- Engage with Shopkeepers: The owners of Çukurcuma's antique shops are often passionate about their collections. Engage with them to learn about the history and provenance of the items on display.

- Plan for Exploration: Çukurcuma is best explored on foot. Wear comfortable shoes and plan for unhurried exploration, allowing yourself the freedom to meander through its narrow lanes.

Modern Marvels: Turkey's Contemporary Scene

Turkey, a land where ancient history and modernity intertwine, is not only a treasure trove of historical wonders but also a dynamic canvas for contemporary life. As you traverse the country, you'll encounter bustling metropolises that pulse with energy, thriving art scenes that blend tradition with innovation, and urban experiences that showcase Turkey's leap into the 21st century. Join us on a journey through modern Turkish cities, exploring their vibrant streets, contemporary art scenes, and the diverse tapestry of experiences that define Turkey's contemporary allure.

1. Istanbul: Where Tradition Meets Trendsetting

Istanbul, the city where East meets west, stands as a testament to the harmonious coexistence of the ancient and the contemporary. As you step into the heart of Istanbul, the juxtaposition of historic landmarks with modern architecture creates a visual spectacle that encapsulates the city's dynamic spirit.

Exploring Istanbul's Modern Marvels:

Istiklal Avenue: Begin your exploration at Istiklal Avenue, the bustling pedestrian street that serves as Istanbul's main modern thoroughfare. Lined with shops, cafes, and galleries, Istiklal Avenue is a microcosm of Istanbul's contemporary scene. Explore modern Turkish fashion in boutique stores, sip coffee at trendy cafes, and immerse yourself in the vibrant street life.

Taksim Square: At the northern end of Istiklal Avenue, Taksim Square emerges as a focal point of modern Istanbul. The square is not only a transportation hub but also a space for gatherings, events, and cultural expressions. Modern sculptures and installations dot the square, offering a glimpse into Istanbul's commitment to public art.

Contemporary Art Museums: Istanbul's art scene has embraced contemporary expressions, and the city is home to several modern art museums. The Istanbul Modern Art Museum, situated along the shores of the Bosphorus, showcases a diverse collection of Turkish and international contemporary art. The Pera Museum, located in the historic district of Beyoğlu, offers a journey through modern and contemporary Turkish art.

Levent and Maslak: Skyscrapers and Business Hubs: Head to the districts of Levent and Maslak to witness Istanbul's modern skyline. Towering skyscrapers house international businesses, financial institutions, and luxury residences. These areas epitomize Istanbul's emergence as a global business hub while providing panoramic views of the city.

Karaköy and Galata: Bohemian Vibes: For a taste of Istanbul's bohemian side, explore the neighbourhoods of Karaköy and Galata. Modern art galleries, design boutiques, and hip cafes contribute to the artistic ambiance of these districts. The Galata Tower, an iconic landmark, offers a panoramic view of the cityscape, blending historic and contemporary perspectives.

Navigational Tips:

- Public Transportation: Istanbul's modern metro and tram systems make navigating the city convenient. Consider getting an Istanbulkart, a smart card that can be used for various modes of public transportation.

- Street Food Exploration: Amidst the modernity, Istanbul's street food scene remains a vibrant link to tradition. Taste local delicacies from street vendors as you stroll through the city's contemporary neighbourhoods.

2. Ankara: The Capital's Modern Core

As the political and administrative capital of Turkey, Ankara stands as a testament to the country's commitment to modern governance and urban planning. While often overshadowed by the historical allure of Istanbul, Ankara boasts its own modern marvels and a thriving contemporary scene.

Exploring Ankara's Modern Marvels:

Atakule Tower: Dominating Ankara's skyline, the Atakule Tower is an iconic symbol of the city's modernity. The tower offers panoramic views of Ankara from its observation deck, providing a unique perspective on the city's layout and architectural landscape.

Gençlik Park: Gençlik Park, meaning Youth Park, is a sprawling green space in the heart of Ankara. The park features modern amenities, including a large pond, walking paths, and recreational areas. It serves as a popular destination for locals seeking outdoor activities and relaxation.

Çıkrıkçılar Yokuşu: Artsy Vibes: To experience Ankara's contemporary art scene, head to Çıkrıkçılar Yokuşu, a street adorned with street art, graffiti, and murals. This vibrant alley is a canvas for local and international artists, providing a dynamic space for creative expression.

Çankaya: Cultural Hub: Explore the Çankaya district, known for its cultural institutions and contemporary lifestyle. Here, you'll find theatres, art galleries, and cultural centres that contribute to Ankara's modern cultural tapestry. The district is also home to trendy cafes, providing a glimpse into Ankara's evolving social scene.

Modern Shopping Centres: Ankara boasts modern shopping centres that cater to diverse tastes. From high-end brands to local boutiques, these centres offer a contemporary shopping experience. Armada Shopping and Entertainment Center and Panora Shopping Center are popular choices for those seeking a mix of retail therapy and entertainment.

Navigational Tips:

- Ankara's Metro System: Ankara's metro system is a convenient way to navigate the city. The Kızılay-Çayyolu metro line, in particular, connects key points in Ankara and provides efficient transportation.

- Cultural Events: Check for cultural events and performances happening in Çankaya and other cultural hubs. Ankara's contemporary arts scene often includes exhibitions, performances, and festivals.

3. Izmir: Aegean Sophistication and Coastal Modernity

Izmir, the pearl of the Aegean, combines coastal charm with modern sophistication. The city's strategic location on the western coast of Turkey has made it a hub of commerce, culture, and contemporary living. From waterfront promenades to bustling markets, Izmir offers a unique blend of tradition and modernity.

Exploring Izmir's Modern Marvels:

Kordon: Seaside Serenity: The Kordon

, Izmir's picturesque waterfront promenade, is a hub of activity and relaxation. Lined with palm trees, cafes, and parks, it's an ideal place for a leisurely stroll. The Kordon showcases Izmir's commitment to creating public spaces that seamlessly blend with the city's natural beauty.

Alsancak: Urban Buzz: Alsancak, one of Izmir's most vibrant neighbourhoods, encapsulates the city's urban energy. Modern cafes, stylish boutiques, and a lively atmosphere characterize this district. The streets of Alsancak come alive in the evening, making it a hotspot for socializing and entertainment.

Asansör: Historical Elegance: Asansör, a historic elevator dating back to the early 20th century, is a symbol of Izmir's cosmopolitan history. The elevator connects the streets of Karataş to the upper neighbourhoods, offering panoramic views of the city and the bay. Today, Asansör is not just a means of transportation but also a popular venue for events and dining.

Kemeraltı Bazaar: While steeped in history, Izmir's Kemeraltı Bazaar has adapted to modern times, becoming a bustling marketplace that combines tradition with contemporary shopping experiences. Explore its narrow alleys to discover a diverse array of shops, from artisanal boutiques to modern concept stores.

Bornova: Education and Innovation Hub: Bornova, home to Ege University, has evolved into a hub of education and innovation. The district hosts cultural events, conferences, and exhibitions that contribute to Izmir's intellectual and creative landscape. Bornova's modern infrastructure reflects the city's commitment to fostering academic and technological advancements.

Navigational Tips:

- Ferry Rides: Take advantage of Izmir's ferry services for a scenic journey across the bay. Ferries connect key points in the city and provide a unique perspective of Izmir's coastal beauty.

- Explore Backstreets: In districts like Alsancak and Bornova, venture into the backstreets to discover hidden gems, including concept stores, art galleries, and local eateries.

4. Antalya: Mediterranean Glamour and Modern Resorts

Antalya, situated on the stunning Mediterranean coast, not only boasts natural beauty but also modern resorts, entertainment complexes, and a thriving tourism scene. The city seamlessly marries the charm of its historic Old Town with the sophistication of contemporary resorts, creating an alluring destination for travellers seeking both relaxation and excitement.

Exploring Antalya's Modern Marvels:

Konyaaltı and Lara Beach: Antalya's coastline is adorned with modern resorts, especially in the districts of Konyaaltı and Lara. These areas feature luxurious hotels, beach clubs, and entertainment venues that cater to visitors seeking a blend of Mediterranean relaxation and contemporary amenities.

Old Town (Kaleiçi): Ancient Charms and Modern Boutiques: While the Old Town (Kaleiçi) is known for its historic architecture and narrow cobblestone streets, it has also embraced modernity. The area is dotted with boutique hotels, trendy cafes, and chic shops that cater to the preferences of modern travellers.

Antalya Aquarium and Entertainment Complex: The Antalya Aquarium is not just an aquatic wonderland; it's a modern entertainment complex that offers a multifaceted experience. Explore the thematic sections, including the Wild Park, Ice World, and Ocean ride XD Cinema, for an immersive journey into marine life and entertainment.

Shopping at TerraCity and MarkAntalya: Antalya's modern shopping centres, such as TerraCity and MarkAntalya, cater to diverse tastes. From international brands to local designers, these centres provide a contemporary shopping experience. TerraCity, in particular, is a lifestyle centre offering not only retail therapy but also dining and entertainment.

Düden Park and Waterfalls: Düden Park, situated along the cliffs overlooking the Mediterranean, combines natural beauty with modern amenities. Explore the park's pathways, enjoy panoramic views, and marvel at the Düden Waterfalls. The park is a popular spot for both locals and tourists seeking a tranquil escape.

Navigational Tips:

- Beach Clubs: In districts like Konyaaltı and Lara, consider spending a day at one of the beach clubs. These modern establishments offer a blend of sun-soaked relaxation, water activities, and vibrant nightlife.

- Old Town Exploration: While wandering through the historic streets of Kaleiçi, keep an eye out for modern boutiques and art galleries that add a contemporary flair to the ancient surroundings.

5. Bodrum: Aegean Sophistication and Bohemian Vibes

Bodrum, with its azure waters, white-washed buildings, and lively atmosphere, has long been a magnet for those seeking a sophisticated yet laid-back escape. The city's modern marinas, boutique hotels, and vibrant nightlife create a captivating blend of Aegean charm and contemporary allure.

Exploring Bodrum's Modern Marvels:

Bodrum Marina: The Bodrum Marina is a testament to the city's allure for yachting enthusiasts and those seeking a taste of luxury. Lined with modern cafes, upscale boutiques, and sleek yachts, the marina is a hub of sophistication. It's an ideal place for a leisurely stroll, people-watching, and enjoying the scenic views.

Halikarnas Nightclub: Bodrum's nightlife is legendary, and at the heart of it is Halikarnas, one of the world's largest open-air nightclubs. With its dazzling light shows, international DJs, and a capacity for thousands of partygoers, Halikarnas encapsulates the city's vibrant and contemporary nightlife scene.

Mausoleum at Halicarnassus: While steeped in ancient history, Bodrum is also home to one of the Seven Wonders of the Ancient World—the Mausoleum at Halicarnassus. The site has been reimagined with modern landscaping and informative displays, allowing visitors to delve into the history of this architectural marvel.

Modern Resorts and Boutique Hotels: Bodrum's coastline is adorned with modern resorts that cater to a range of tastes, from family-friendly establishments to exclusive boutique hotels. These resorts often feature sleek designs, infinity pools, and panoramic views of the Aegean Sea.

Bodrum Amphitheatre: The Bodrum Amphitheatre, dating back to the Hellenistic period, has undergone restoration to ensure its preservation. Today, it serves as a venue for concerts, cultural events, and performances, blending ancient history with contemporary cultural expressions.

Navigational Tips:

- Bohemian Exploration: In districts like Bodrum's Old Town and Türkbükü, embrace the bohemian vibes. Explore boutique shops, art galleries, and beachside cafes for a taste of Bodrum's eclectic character.

- Yachting Excursions: Consider a yachting excursion along the Aegean coast. Bodrum's modern marinas provide opportunities to charter yachts for day trips or longer voyages.

Getting Around: Transportation Tips in Turkey

Turkey, with its rich tapestry of landscapes, historic sites, and vibrant cities, beckons travellers to embark on a journey of discovery. Navigating this diverse country requires an understanding of its transportation networks, which seamlessly connect bustling metropolises, ancient ruins, and picturesque coastlines. From the efficient bus system to the scenic train routes and the convenience of domestic flights, this comprehensive guide will equip you with the knowledge to explore Turkey's wonders with ease.

1. Buses: The Pulse of Turkish Transportation

Buses are the backbone of Turkey's transportation system, providing a cost-effective and extensive network that connects cities, towns, and even remote villages. Whether you're traversing the Anatolian plateau or winding through coastal roads, buses offer a comfortable and immersive way to experience the country.

Types of Buses:

Intercity Buses (Şehirlerarası Otobüs): These buses connect major cities and towns across Turkey. They vary in comfort, with options ranging from standard to luxury buses equipped with amenities like Wi-Fi and personal entertainment screens.

Local Buses (Belediye Otobüsü): Operating within cities, local buses are an economical mode of transportation for short distances. They are essential for exploring urban centres and reaching neighbourhoods not served by the metro or tram.

Dolmuş: A shared minibus or minivan, the dolmuş follows specific routes within cities and towns. Passengers can hop on and off along the route, and payment is typically made to the driver upon exiting.

Turkish State Railways (TCDD) Buses: Complementing the train network, TCDD buses connect cities and towns that may not be directly serviced by the rail system. They are especially useful for reaching destinations off the main rail routes.

Navigating Bus Travel:

Booking Tickets: Intercity bus tickets can be purchased online through various platforms or at bus terminals (otogar). For popular routes or during peak travel times, it's advisable to book tickets in advance. Local buses and dolmuş generally accept payment on board.

Otogars: Bus terminals, known as otogar, are well-organized hubs with ticket offices, waiting areas, and amenities like cafes and restrooms. Major cities have central otogars, and smaller towns may have more modest terminals.

Comfort Levels: Intercity buses come in different comfort classes, including standard, business, and luxury. Consider your preferences and budget when choosing a class. Business and luxury classes often provide more spacious seating, refreshments, and entertainment options.

Dolmuş Etiquette: When taking a dolmuş, signal the driver by waving your hand to stop. Pay the fare to the driver upon exiting. It's common for passengers to pass money to the driver via others if they're seated far from the front.

Useful Phrases:

- "Otobüs nerede?" – Where is the bus?

- "Ne kadar?" – How much is it?

- "İnerken ödemek istiyorum." – I want to pay when getting off.

2. Trains: Scenic Journeys through Anatolia

Turkey's rail network offers travellers the chance to embark on scenic journeys through diverse landscapes, from the lush greenery of the Black Sea region to the arid beauty of Central Anatolia. While the train network is not as extensive as the bus system, it provides a comfortable and leisurely mode of transportation.

Key Train Routes:

Ankara to Istanbul (Yüksek Hızlı Tren - YHT): The high-speed train between Ankara and Istanbul is a popular route, connecting the country's capital with its largest city in around four hours. Enjoy panoramic views of the Turkish countryside while traveling at high speeds.

Eastern Express (Doğu Ekspresi): This iconic route runs from Ankara to Kars, traversing the Anatolian plateau and reaching the easternmost parts of Turkey. The journey is known for its breath-taking scenery, including snow-capped mountains and pristine landscapes.

South Express (Güney Ekspresi): The South Express travels from Ankara to Kurtalan, passing through picturesque towns and providing a glimpse into rural life in southern Turkey.

Coast Starlight (Mavi Tren): The Mavi Tren operates along the Mediterranean and Aegean coasts, connecting İzmir to Adana. Passengers can enjoy views of the turquoise waters of the Aegean Sea and the historical sites dotting the coast.

Navigating Train Travel:

Ticket Reservations: Train tickets can be purchased online through the official website of the Turkish State Railways (TCDD) or at train stations. For popular routes, especially during peak travel seasons, it's advisable to book tickets in advance.

Classes of Service: Trains offer different classes of service, including pulman (standard), kuşetli (couchette), and yatakli (sleeper). The type of service available depends on the specific train and route. Sleeper cars are available on long-distance routes.

Train Stations: Train stations (gar) are well-equipped with ticket offices, waiting areas, and facilities like cafes and restrooms. Larger stations also have luggage storage services. Check the station's timetable for train departures and arrivals.

Scenic Stops: Some train routes include scenic stops, allowing passengers to disembark, explore, and re-join a later train. For example, the Eastern Express has a popular stop in Erzurum, allowing passengers to visit historical sites.

Useful Phrases:

- "Tren nereden kalkıyor?" – Where does the train depart from?

- "Bilet ne kadar?" – How much is the ticket?

- "Hangi perondan kalkıyor?" – Which platform does it depart from?

3. Domestic Flights: Wings across the Skies

Turkey's geographical expanse makes domestic flights an efficient way to cover long distances, especially between major cities and tourist destinations. With a well-developed aviation sector, domestic flights offer convenience and time efficiency for travellers exploring different regions of the country.

Key Domestic Airlines:

Turkish Airlines (THY): As the flagship carrier of Turkey, Turkish Airlines operates an extensive network of domestic flights, connecting major cities and regional airports. The airline is known for its high-quality service and frequent schedules.

Pegasus Airlines: Pegasus is a low-cost carrier that serves various domestic and international destinations. It offers budget-friendly options for travellers looking to cover long distances quickly.

AnadoluJet: A subsidiary of Turkish Airlines, AnadoluJet focuses on domestic flights, providing connections to cities and towns across Anatolia. It caters to both business and leisure travellers.

Navigating Domestic Flights:

Airport Choices: Major cities like Istanbul and Ankara have multiple airports. Check the departure and arrival airports, as well as their locations, to ensure seamless travel. For example, Istanbul has two airports, Istanbul Airport (IST) and Sabiha Gökçen International Airport (SAW).

Booking Flights: Domestic flights can be booked online through airline websites or third-party platforms. It's advisable to book in advance, especially during peak travel seasons. Turkish Airlines and Pegasus Airlines often offer competitive prices.

Check-In Procedures: Check-in for domestic flights can be done online or at the airport. Airlines usually allow online check-in up to 24 hours before the flight. At the airport, proceed to the check-in counters or use self-check-in kiosks.

Security and Boarding: Domestic flights in Turkey involve security checks similar to international flights. Ensure compliance with security regulations, and arrive at the airport with sufficient time for security procedures. Boarding typically begins well in advance of the departure time.

Useful Phrases:

- "Uçağım ne zaman kalkıyor?" – When does my flight depart?

- "Hangi terminalden?" – From which terminal?

- "Yerim nerede?" – Where is my seat?

4. Shared Taxis and Minibuses: Local Journeys

For short distances within cities or towns, shared taxis (dolmuş) and minibuses are common modes of transportation. These are flexible and affordable options for reaching destinations not easily accessible by standard public transportation.

Dolmuş and Minibus Tips:

Flexible Routes: Dolmuş and minibuses operate on set routes within cities or towns. They pick up passengers along the way and drop them off at requested locations. Routes are often displayed on the front of the vehicle.

Fare Payment: Payment for dolmuş and minibuses is usually made to the driver upon exiting. The fare is fixed and typically reasonable, making these modes of transport accessible for short journeys.

Destination Inquiry: If you're unsure whether a dolmuş or minibus travels to your desired destination, ask the driver or fellow passengers. Locals are often helpful in providing information about routes and stops.

Popular Routes: Dolmuş and minibuses are particularly useful for reaching neighbourhoods, markets, and attractions not directly served by larger buses or metro lines. They offer a convenient way to explore local areas.

Useful Phrases:

- "Dolmuş nereden kalkıyor?" – Where does the dolmuş depart from?

- "Buradan kaça?" – How much is it from here?

- "Beni burada bırakabilir misiniz?" – Can you drop me off here?

5. Rental Cars: Freedom on the Road

For travellers seeking the freedom to explore at their own pace, renting a car is a popular option in Turkey. The country's well-maintained road network and diverse landscapes make road trips an exciting and flexible way to discover hidden gems.

Rental Car Tips:

International Driving Permit: While not mandatory, having an International Driving Permit (IDP) is advisable for renting a car in Turkey. It's a translation of your driver's license and may be required by rental companies.

Road Signs and Traffic Rules: Familiarize yourself with Turkish road signs and traffic rules before embarking on a road trip. This includes understanding speed limits, road markings, and right-of-way rules.

Fuel Stations: Turkey has an extensive network of fuel stations along major highways and in urban areas. Most stations accept credit cards. Consider filling up the tank when leaving cities, as rural areas may have fewer options.

Parking: Urban areas have designated parking areas, and street parking may require a fee. In tourist destinations, look for secure parking lots. When exploring rural areas or historic sites, inquire about parking options.

GPS Navigation: While major roads are well-signposted, having a GPS navigation system or a mobile navigation app can be helpful, especially for rural routes or less-travelled areas.

Useful Phrases:

- "Araç kiralamak istiyorum." – I want to rent a car.

- "Yol tarifi alabilir miyim?" – Can I get directions?

- "Benzin istasyonu nerede?" – Where is the gas station?

6. Ferries: Island Hopping and Coastal Crossings

Turkey's strategic location between Europe and Asia, coupled with its extensive coastline, makes ferries a popular mode of transportation for island hopping and coastal journeys. Ferries connect major cities, historical sites, and picturesque islands, providing a unique perspective of the country.

Ferry Travel Tips:

Bosphorus Ferries: In Istanbul, ferries traverse the Bosphorus, connecting the European and Asian sides of the city. This scenic journey offers breath-taking views of Istanbul's iconic skyline and historic landmarks.

Aegean and Mediterranean Ferries: Coastal regions like the Aegean and Mediterranean boast ferry routes that connect mainland Turkey to islands and peninsulas. From Çeşme to Chios or Bodrum to Kos, ferries offer a leisurely way to explore these coastal gems.

Booking Tickets: Ferry tickets can be purchased online, at ferry terminals, or through travel agencies. During peak travel seasons or for popular routes, consider booking tickets in advance, especially for car ferries.

Schedules and Routes: Ferry schedules vary, and some routes may only operate seasonally. Check the ferry company's website or inquire at ferry terminals for the latest information on schedules and routes.

Comfort on Board: Ferries range from standard vessels to high-speed catamarans and luxurious cruise-style boats. Depending on the route and duration, choose a ferry that suits your preferences for comfort and amenities.

Useful Phrases:

- "Feribot nereden kalkıyor?" – Where does the ferry depart from?

- "Bilet ne kadar?" – How much is the ticket?

- "Hangi saatte var?" – What time does it depart?

7. Walking and Cycling: Exploring on Foot and by Bike

For a more intimate exploration of cities, towns, and natural wonders, walking and cycling provide a refreshing alternative to motorized transportation. Many Turkish cities are pedestrian-friendly, and dedicated cycling paths are emerging in urban areas and along scenic routes.

Tips for Walking and Cycling:

City Exploration: In historic districts and city centres, walking is often the best way to explore. Wander through narrow alleys, discover hidden gems, and soak in the local atmosphere on foot.

Cycling Paths: Some cities, including Istanbul and Izmir, have developed cycling paths along waterfronts and green spaces. Renting a bike or bringing your own allows you to enjoy the scenery while staying active.

Guided Walking Tours: Joining guided walking tours in cities like Istanbul or Cappadocia provides insights into local history, culture, and architecture. Knowledgeable guides can enhance your understanding of the places you visit.

Rural Exploration: In rural areas or near natural landmarks, walking and hiking trails offer opportunities to connect with nature. From the Lycian Way along the Mediterranean to the trails of Cappadocia, Turkey is a haven for hikers.

Useful Phrases:

- "Yürüyerek ne kadar sürer?" – How long does it take to walk there?

- "Bisiklet kiralayabilir miyim?" – Can I rent a bike?

- "Yakındaki park nerede?" – Where is the nearby park?

Health and Safety: Essential Guidelines for Traveling in Turkey

Embarking on a journey to Turkey promises a tapestry of cultural experiences, historical wonders, and breath-taking landscapes. As you traverse the country's diverse regions, it's crucial to prioritize your health and safety. This comprehensive guide provides essential information on healthcare, safety precautions, and the importance of travel insurance to ensure your travels are not only memorable but also secure.

1. Healthcare in Turkey: A Mosaic of Services

Turkey boasts a robust healthcare system, blending modern medical facilities with traditional practices. Whether you require medical attention in a bustling city or a remote village, the country's healthcare infrastructure strives to meet international standards. Understanding the healthcare landscape and taking proactive measures can contribute to a safe and enjoyable travel experience.

Medical Facilities:

Hospitals: Major cities, including Istanbul, Ankara, and Izmir, are equipped with state-of-the-art hospitals offering a wide range of medical services. University hospitals, such as those affiliated with medical schools, often have English-speaking staff and international standards of care.

Clinics: In urban and tourist areas, you'll find private clinics specializing in various medical fields. These clinics are adept at handling both routine and emergency medical issues.

Pharmacies (Eczane): Pharmacies are widespread in cities and towns, and pharmacists are highly trained. They can provide advice on common ailments, dispense medications, and guide you to appropriate medical facilities if needed.

Emergency Services: Turkey has a well-established emergency medical response system. In case of a medical emergency, dial 112 for an ambulance. Major cities also have private ambulance services.

Essential Health Tips:

Travel Insurance: Before embarking on your journey, securing comprehensive travel insurance is essential. This includes coverage for medical emergencies, trip cancellations, and travel-related mishaps. Confirm that your insurance covers activities you plan to engage in, such as adventure sports or hiking.

Vaccinations: Routine vaccinations, including measles, mumps, rubella, diphtheria, tetanus, and pertussis, should be up-to-date. Depending on your travel plans, additional vaccinations such as Hepatitis A and B, and typhoid may be recommended. Consult your healthcare provider well in advance.

Prescription Medications: If you are on prescription medications, ensure an adequate supply for the duration of your trip. Carry a copy of your prescriptions and, if possible, a letter from your healthcare provider explaining your medical condition and the necessity of the medications.

Water and Food Safety: While tap water in urban areas is generally safe for drinking, it's advisable to stick to bottled or purified water, especially in rural areas. Avoid consuming raw or undercooked foods, and opt for freshly prepared meals in reputable establishments.

Sun Protection: Turkey experiences a Mediterranean climate, and sun exposure can be intense, particularly in summer. Use sunscreen, wear a hat, and stay hydrated to protect yourself from the sun's rays.

2. Safety Precautions: Navigating Urban and Rural Landscapes

Ensuring your safety during your travels involves a combination of awareness, preparation, and adherence to local customs. Turkey is known for its hospitality, but like any destination, it's wise to stay vigilant and take precautions to safeguard yourself and your belongings.

Urban Safety Tips:

Crowded Areas: Popular tourist destinations, markets, and transportation hubs may be crowded. Be mindful of your belongings, use anti-theft accessories like money belts, and keep valuables secure. Be cautious of pickpockets, especially in crowded areas.

Transportation Safety: Exercise caution when using public transportation, especially in urban centres. Keep an eye on your belongings, use reliable transportation services, and be aware of your surroundings. Taxis with official markings are generally safe.

Street Crossing: Traffic can be hectic in urban areas. Use designated crosswalks, follow pedestrian signals, and be cautious when crossing streets. In cities like Istanbul, where the traffic flow may be intense, utilize pedestrian underpasses or overpasses when available.

Night Safety: While many areas are safe to explore at night, it's advisable to stay in well-lit and populated areas. Avoid poorly lit or isolated streets, and use reliable transportation services, especially late at night.

Emergency Contacts: Familiarize yourself with emergency contact numbers, including the local police (155) and tourism police (tourism police offices are available in major tourist destinations). Keep a copy of your identification, passport, and emergency contacts in a secure location.

Rural Safety Tips:

Outdoor Activities: Turkey's diverse landscapes beckon outdoor enthusiasts. Whether you're hiking in Cappadocia, exploring ancient ruins, or enjoying coastal walks, be prepared with suitable footwear, maps, and, if necessary, a guide. Inform someone about your plans if venturing into less-travelled areas.

Wildlife Awareness: In rural and natural areas, be aware of local wildlife, especially if engaging in activities like camping or hiking. Keep a safe distance and avoid approaching or feeding wild animals. Familiarize yourself with potential risks in specific regions, such as encounters with snakes or insects.

Cultural Sensitivity: In rural communities, respect local customs and traditions. Seek permission before photographing individuals, especially in conservative areas. Dress modestly when visiting religious or rural sites.

Weather Preparedness: Turkey's diverse climate can bring unexpected weather changes. Whether exploring the mountains or coastal areas, be prepared for sudden shifts in temperature, rain, or wind. Check weather forecasts and plan accordingly.

Communication Challenges: In remote areas, language barriers may be more pronounced. Consider learning basic Turkish phrases or using translation apps to facilitate communication. Local communities often appreciate efforts to engage in their language.

3. Travel Insurance: A Safety Net for Your Journey

Travel insurance is a crucial aspect of trip planning that provides a safety net in case of unforeseen events. While no one anticipates emergencies or disruptions during their travels, having comprehensive coverage can mitigate financial burdens and ensure a smoother resolution to unexpected situations.

Components of Travel Insurance:

Medical Coverage: The primary function of travel insurance is to cover medical expenses in case of illness or injury during your trip. This includes hospital stays, doctor visits, and emergency medical evacuation if necessary.

Trip Cancellation or Interruption: Travel insurance often covers non-refundable trip costs in case of cancellations or interruptions due to unforeseen circumstances such as illness, natural disasters, or emergencies.

Travel Delays and Missed Connections: If your travel plans are disrupted due to delays or missed connections, travel insurance can provide coverage for additional expenses incurred, such as accommodation and meals.

Lost or Stolen Belongings: Coverage for lost, stolen, or damaged luggage and personal belongings is a standard feature of travel insurance. This includes reimbursement for the cost of replacing essential items.

Emergency Evacuation and Repatriation: In the event of a medical emergency, travel insurance can cover the costs of emergency evacuation to the nearest adequate medical facility or repatriation to your home country.

Choosing the Right Travel Insurance:

Coverage Limits: Review the coverage limits for medical expenses, trip cancellation, and other components. Ensure that the coverage aligns with your travel plans and needs.

Adventure Activities: If you plan to engage in adventure sports or activities, confirm that your travel insurance covers these pursuits. Some activities may require additional coverage.

Pre-existing Conditions: Declare any pre-existing medical conditions when purchasing travel insurance. Some policies may exclude coverage for pre-existing conditions unless disclosed.

Policy Exclusions: Understand the exclusions and limitations of the policy. Common exclusions may include acts of war, civil unrest, and certain natural disasters. Be aware of any restrictions that may apply.

Duration and Frequency: Select a policy that aligns with the duration of your trip and consider annual multi-trip policies if you are a frequent traveller.

Emergency Assistance Services: Check if the travel insurance provider offers 24/7 emergency assistance services. This can be invaluable in coordinating medical care, providing travel advice, and assisting in emergencies.

Claim Procedures: Familiarize yourself with the claims process, including required documentation and procedures. Keep a copy of your insurance policy and emergency contact details easily accessible during your travels.

4. Local Health and Safety Considerations: Cultural Sensitivity

Respecting local customs and adhering to cultural norms not only enhances your travel experience but also contributes to a harmonious and respectful interaction with the communities you encounter. Turkey, with its rich cultural heritage and diverse traditions, appreciates visitors who approach its customs with an open mind and cultural sensitivity.

Cultural Considerations:

Dress Modestly: In conservative regions and religious sites, dress modestly as a sign of respect. Women may be required to cover their heads or shoulders, and men may be expected to dress formally in certain settings.

Greetings and Politeness: Greet locals with common Turkish phrases like "Merhaba" (Hello) and "Teşekkür ederim" (Thank you). Demonstrating politeness and courtesy is highly valued in Turkish culture.

Removing Shoes: In many Turkish homes, it is customary to remove shoes before entering. Be attentive to cues from your hosts, and consider bringing clean socks if you plan on visiting homes.

Haggling at Markets: Bargaining is a common practice in Turkish markets and bazaars. While negotiating, maintain a friendly and respectful tone. Recognize the cultural significance of haggling as a social exchange.

Respect for Religious Sites: When visiting mosques, churches, or other religious sites, follow established guidelines. Dress modestly, remove your shoes when required, and maintain a quiet and respectful demeanor.

Photography Etiquette: Always ask for permission before photographing individuals, especially in rural areas. Respect the privacy of locals and be mindful of cultural sensitivities.

Language Considerations:

Basic Turkish Phrases: While English is widely spoken in tourist areas, learning a few basic Turkish phrases can go a long way in enhancing your interactions. Locals appreciate the effort, and it fosters a more immersive experience.

- "Merhaba" – Hello

- "Teşekkür ederim" – Thank you

- "Evet" – Yes

- "Hayır" – No

- "Lütfen" – Please

- "Görüşürüz" – Goodbye

Understanding Social Customs: Turks are known for their warm hospitality. It's common to be invited into homes for tea or meals. Accept such invitations graciously, and reciprocate the hospitality if possible.

Friday Prayer: On Fridays, the Muslim holy day, some businesses and public offices may close during Friday prayers. Plan your activities accordingly, and be aware of the cultural significance of this day.

Health and Dietary Considerations:

Turkish Cuisine: Embrace the opportunity to savour Turkey's rich culinary heritage. Turkish cuisine includes a variety of dishes, from kebabs to mezes (appetizers) and traditional sweets. Be open to trying local specialties.

Water and Beverages: While tap water in urban areas is generally safe, it's advisable to drink bottled or purified water, especially in rural regions. Turkish tea (çay) is a popular beverage, and hospitality often involves offering guests tea.

Special Dietary Requirements: If you have specific dietary requirements or allergies, communicate these clearly when ordering food. Turkish cuisine can be adapted to accommodate various preferences.

Street Food Hygiene: Street food is an integral part of Turkish culinary culture. Choose vendors with clean and well-maintained stalls. Hot, freshly prepared items are often safer choices.

5. Emergencies and Local Assistance: Contacts and Resources

Being prepared for emergencies involves knowing local emergency contacts, understanding available resources, and having access to information that can aid you in unexpected situations. Familiarize yourself with key contacts and resources to ensure a swift response to any issues that may arise during your travels.

Emergency Contacts:

Medical Emergency: Dial 112 for emergency medical assistance. The operator can dispatch an ambulance to your location. This number is toll-free and operates 24/7.

Police Assistance: In case of criminal incidents or emergencies requiring police intervention, dial 155 to reach the local police. Provide details of the situation and your location.

Tourism Police: Major tourist destinations have dedicated tourism police offices. The tourism police can assist with issues related to tourists, including lost documents or reporting incidents. Check local directories for the nearest office.

Consular Assistance: If you are a foreign national and require assistance from your embassy or consulate, keep the contact information for your country's diplomatic mission in Turkey. Consular services can assist with issues such as lost passports or emergencies.

Local Resources:

Pharmacies: Pharmacies (eczane) are widespread in urban and rural areas. In cities, many pharmacies operate 24/7 on a rotating basis to provide emergency services. Look for the sign "Eczane Nöbetçi" to find the nearest open pharmacy.

Hospitals and Clinics: Major cities have well-equipped hospitals and clinics. For non-emergency medical issues, you can visit private clinics or university hospitals with international standards of care.

Language Assistance: In case of language barriers, translation apps or phrasebooks can be valuable resources. Additionally, many hotels, tourist information centres, and transportation hubs have English-speaking staff.

Local Tourist Information Centres: Tourist information centres in major cities and tourist destinations provide maps, brochures, and assistance. They can offer guidance on local attractions, transportation, and safety.

Travel Apps and Resources:

Emergency Apps: Install emergency apps that provide real-time information on local emergencies, natural disasters, and security updates. These apps can be valuable tools for staying informed.

Translation Apps: Apps that facilitate language translation can be invaluable, especially in areas where English may not be widely spoken. Translate phrases or questions to enhance communication.

Navigation Apps: Utilize navigation apps to navigate cities, find local attractions, and plan routes. Some apps offer offline maps, which can be helpful in areas with limited connectivity.

Local News Sources: Stay informed about local news and events by accessing local news websites or using news apps. Awareness of current events can contribute to your overall safety.

6. Conclusion: Navigating Turkey with Confidence

Embarking on a journey through Turkey is a captivating adventure filled with cultural richness, historical marvels, and natural beauty. By prioritizing health and safety, you can navigate the diverse landscapes and urban hubs with confidence, ensuring that your travels are not only enriching but also secure.

Planning Your Trip: Itinerary Suggestions for Every Travel Style

Embarking on a journey to Turkey is an immersive experience that offers a rich tapestry of history, culture, and natural beauty. From the bustling bazaars of Istanbul to the ancient ruins of Ephesus, and the serene beaches along the Mediterranean coast, Turkey caters to a diverse range of travel styles. Whether you're a history enthusiast, an adventure seeker, or a beach lover, this comprehensive guide provides sample itineraries tailored to different travel preferences.

1. The Historical Odyssey: A Journey through Time

For those enchanted by the echoes of the past, Turkey's historical sites are a treasure trove waiting to be explored. This itinerary takes you on a chronological journey, visiting iconic landmarks that span centuries of civilization.

Day 1-3: Istanbul - Where East Meets West

Day 1: Sultanahmet District

- Morning: Begin your historical odyssey at the Hagia Sophia, a marvel of Byzantine architecture. Explore its vast interior, adorned with stunning mosaics.

- Afternoon: Visit the Blue Mosque, known for its blue tiles and intricate calligraphy. Enjoy a stroll through Sultanahmet Square, surrounded by historical sites.

- Evening: Wander through the Grand Bazaar, a labyrinth of shops offering traditional Turkish crafts and souvenirs.

Day 2: Topkapi Palace and Archaeology Museum

- Morning: Delve into the opulent Topkapi Palace, once the residence of Ottoman sultans. Explore the Harem, Imperial Council, and Treasury.

- Afternoon: Visit the Istanbul Archaeology Museums, housing a vast collection of artefacts from different eras, including the famous Alexander Sarcophagus.

- Evening: Enjoy a cruise along the Bosphorus to witness Istanbul's skyline illuminated at night.

Day 3: Chora Church and Fener-Balat

- Morning: Explore the Chora Church (Kariye Museum), renowned for its stunning Byzantine mosaics and frescoes.

- Afternoon: Venture into the Fener-Balat districts, known for their historic Greek and Jewish quarters. Visit the Church of St. George and colourful houses along the Golden Horn.

- Evening: Sample local cuisine at a traditional meyhane (Turkish tavern) in the lively Beyoğlu district.

Day 4-6: Ephesus - A Glimpse of Ancient Glory

Day 4: Ephesus Archaeological Site

- Morning: Fly to Izmir and head to Ephesus, one of the best-preserved ancient cities. Begin your exploration at the Celsus Library and the Grand Theatre.

- Afternoon: Visit the Terrace Houses, showcasing well-preserved Roman villas with intricate frescoes and mosaics.

- Evening: Relax in the charming town of Selçuk and enjoy local cuisine.

Day 5: Ephesus Museum and Sirince Village

- Morning: Explore the Ephesus Archaeological Museum to see artefacts unearthed from the ancient city.

- Afternoon: Visit the picturesque village of Şirince, known for its cobblestone streets, traditional houses, and fruit wines.

- Evening: Return to Selçuk for a quiet evening in this historical town.

Day 6: Priene, Miletus, and Didyma

- Full Day Excursion: Explore the ancient cities of Priene, Miletus, and Didyma. Marvel at the well-preserved Temple of Apollo in Didyma and the theatre in Miletus.

- Evening: Return to Selçuk for a farewell dinner.

Day 7-9: Cappadocia - Fairy Chimneys and Cave Dwellings

Day 7: Goreme Open-Air Museum

- Morning: Fly to Cappadocia and start your journey in the Goreme Open-Air Museum, a UNESCO World Heritage site with cave churches and frescoes.

- Afternoon: Explore the surreal landscapes of Devrent Valley and Pasabag (Monks Valley).

- Evening: Relax in a cave hotel and enjoy a traditional Turkish dinner.

Day 8: Hot Air Balloon Ride and Underground Cities

- Morning: Experience the magic of Cappadocia with a sunrise hot air balloon ride.

- Afternoon: Discover the underground cities of Kaymaklı or Derinkuyu, impressive complexes carved into the rock.

- Evening: Savour a Turkish night show with traditional music and dance.

Day 9: Ihlara Valley and Uchisar Castle

- Full Day Excursion: Hike in the stunning Ihlara Valley, dotted with rock-cut churches. Visit Uchisar Castle for panoramic views of Cappadocia.

- Evening: Farewell dinner in a cave restaurant.

2. Adventure Seeker's Delight: Thrills in Nature and Beyond

For those who crave excitement and outdoor exploration, Turkey's diverse landscapes offer a playground for adventure. From hiking in the rugged mountains to diving in crystal-clear waters, this itinerary satisfies the adrenaline seeker's appetite.

Day 1-3: Antalya - Gateway to the Turquoise Coast

Day 1: Old Town and Harbour

- Morning: Arrive in Antalya and explore the charming Old Town (Kaleiçi) with its narrow streets, Ottoman houses, and historical sites.

- Afternoon: Stroll along the picturesque harbour and visit the Antalya Archaeological Museum.

- Evening: Enjoy dinner at a seaside restaurant.

Day 2: White Water Rafting and Olympos

- Full Day Excursion: Experience white-water rafting on the Köprülü River. After the adventure, head to the coastal village of Olympos.

- Evening: Relax on the beach and stay in a tree house or a beachfront bungalow.

Day 3: Chimera Flames and Lycian Way

- Morning: Hike to the eternal flames of Chimera, a natural phenomenon of burning gas vents.

- Afternoon: Explore a section of the Lycian Way, a long-distance hiking trail with breath-taking views.

- Evening: Share stories around a campfire in Olympos.

Day 4-6: Fethiye - The Adventure Continues

Day 4: Paragliding and Blue Lagoon

- Morning: Soar above the turquoise coast with a paragliding experience from Babadağ Mountain.

- Afternoon: Relax at the Blue Lagoon in Ölüdeniz, known for its crystal-clear waters and scenic beauty.

- Evening: Enjoy a seafood dinner in Fethiye.

Day 5: Saklikent Gorge and Canyoning

- Full Day Excursion: Head to Saklikent Gorge for canyoning adventures in its icy waters. Explore the gorge's stunning landscapes.

- Evening: Return to Fethiye for a well-deserved rest.

Day 6: Butterfly Valley and Boat Trip

- Morning: Take a boat trip to Butterfly Valley, a secluded beach surrounded by cliffs.

- Afternoon: Enjoy snorkelling, swimming, and sunbathing on the boat trip.

- Evening: Farewell dinner in Fethiye.

Day 7-9: Cappadocia - Land of Fairy Chimneys

Day 7: ATV Tour and Underground Cities

- Morning: Explore Cappadocia's unique landscapes with an ATV tour, passing through valleys and fairy chimneys.

- Afternoon: Visit one of the underground cities, such as Kaymaklı, for an underground adventure.

- Evening: Relax in a cave hotel and enjoy local cuisine.

Day 8: Hot Air Balloon Ride and Hiking

- Morning: Soar above Cappadocia in a hot air balloon for breath-taking views of the sunrise.

- Afternoon: Hike in the scenic Rose Valley or Love Valley.

- Evening: Traditional Turkish night show.

Day 9: Horseback Riding and Pottery Workshop

- Morning: Explore Cappadocia on horseback, riding through valleys and villages.

- Afternoon: Try your hand at traditional pottery with a workshop in Avanos.

- Evening: Farewell dinner in a cave restaurant.

3. The Leisurely Coastal Retreat: Sun, Sea, and Relaxation

For those seeking sun-soaked beaches, tranquil waters, and leisurely strolls along the coastline, Turkey's Mediterranean and Aegean coasts offer the perfect escape. This itinerary combines beachside bliss with cultural discoveries.

Day 1-3: Bodrum - A Maritime Haven

Day 1: Bodrum Castle and Marina

- Morning: Arrive in Bodrum and explore Bodrum Castle, home to the Museum of Underwater Archaeology.

- Afternoon: Stroll along the Bodrum Marina, lined with cafes, shops, and boutiques.

- Evening: Enjoy a seafood dinner with a view of the castle.

Day 2: Boat Trip to Karaada Island

- Full Day Excursion: Take a boat trip to Karaada Island, known for its healing thermal waters. Relax in the natural hot springs.

- Evening: Sunset dinner cruise along the coast.

Day 3: Ancient Theatre and Mausoleum

- Morning: Visit the ancient theatre of Bodrum, offering panoramic views of the city and sea.

- Afternoon: Explore the Mausoleum at Halicarnassus, one of the Seven Wonders of the Ancient World.

- Evening: Sample Turkish mezes at a seaside restaurant.

Day 4-6: Kas - Seaside Serenity

Day 4: Lycian Way and Amphitheatre

- Morning: Transfer to Kas and start your exploration with a walk along the Lycian Way, offering stunning coastal views.

- Afternoon: Discover the ancient amphitheatre in Kas and relax at a seaside cafe.

- Evening: Enjoy dinner in the charming town centre.

Day 5: Sunken City of Kekova and Simena Castle

- Full Day Excursion: Take a boat trip to the Sunken City of Kekova and explore the ruins submerged in crystal-clear waters. Visit Simena Castle for panoramic views.

- Evening: Return to Kas for a quiet evening.

Day 6: Beach Day and Local Cuisine

- Morning: Relax on one of Kas's beautiful beaches, such as Kaputas Beach or Big Pebble Beach.

- Afternoon: Stroll through the town's narrow streets, filled with shops and cafes.

- Evening: Farewell dinner at a seaside restaurant.

Day 7-9: Antalya - The Mediterranean Gem

Day 7: Antalya Old Town and Hadrian's Gate

- Morning: Return to Antalya and explore the picturesque Old Town. Visit Hadrian's Gate and the Clock Tower.

- Afternoon: Wander through the vibrant streets and shop for souvenirs.

- Evening: Dinner at a traditional Turkish restaurant.

Day 8: Duden Waterfalls and Perge

- Morning: Visit the Lower Duden Waterfalls, a natural wonder near Antalya.

- Afternoon: Explore the ancient city of Perge, known for its well-preserved ruins, including a stadium and agora.

- Evening: Relax at a seaside cafe in Antalya.

Day 9: Relaxation and Departure

- Morning: Enjoy a leisurely morning, perhaps with a visit to the Antalya Aquarium or a final stroll along the beach.

- Afternoon: Depart from Antalya, carrying the memories of a tranquil coastal retreat.

4. The Culinary Expedition: A Gastronomic Tour of Turkey

For food enthusiasts eager to savour the diverse flavours of Turkish cuisine, this itinerary takes you on a gastronomic journey, from bustling food markets to traditional eateries.

Day 1-3: Istanbul - A Culinary Melting Pot

Day 1: Spice Bazaar and Street Food

- Morning: Begin your culinary adventure at the Spice Bazaar, where vibrant stalls offer a kaleidoscope of spices, nuts, and sweets.

- Afternoon: Sample Istanbul's street food, including simit (sesame-seed bread), kebabs, and Turkish delight.

- Evening: Enjoy a traditional Turkish dinner at a local restaurant.

Day 2: Cooking Class and Local Markets

- Morning: Participate in a Turkish cooking class, learning to prepare dishes like mezes, kebabs, and baklava.

- Afternoon: Explore local markets, such as Kadikoy Market on the Asian side, known for its fresh produce and seafood.

- Evening: Savour your own creations at the cooking class.

Day 3: Bosphorus Cruise and Seafood Feast

- Morning: Take a Bosphorus cruise, enjoying views of historical landmarks. Visit the fish market in Ortakoy.

- Afternoon: Indulge in a seafood feast at a waterside restaurant.

- Evening: Relax with a cup of Turkish tea or coffee at a traditional teahouse.

Day 4-6: Gaziantep - Culinary Capital of Turkey

Day 4: Gaziantep Old Town and Baklava Tasting

- Morning: Fly to Gaziantep and explore the city's charming old town, known for its historic architecture.

- Afternoon: Sample Gaziantep's famous baklava at renowned local patisseries.

- Evening: Dinner at a traditional kebab restaurant.

Day 5: Culinary Walking Tour and Mosaic Museum

- Morning: Join a culinary walking tour, tasting local specialties like lahmacun (Turkish pizza) and kebabs.

- Afternoon: Visit the Zeugma Mosaic Museum, home to an extensive collection of Roman mosaics.

- Evening: Relish an authentic Gaziantep dinner with regional dishes.

Day 6: Olive Oil Museum and Pistachio Delights

- Morning: Explore the Olive Oil Museum, learning about the production of olive oil in the region.

- Afternoon: Savour Gaziantep's famed pistachio delights, including baklava and künefe.

- Evening: Farewell dinner with Gaziantep's culinary delights.

Day 7-9: Izmir

Conclusion: A Journey to Remember - Unveiling the Tapestry of Turkey's Charms

As your journey through Turkey draws to a close, you find yourself wrapped in a tapestry of experiences that span ancient history, vibrant culture, breath-taking landscapes, and warm hospitality. From the bustling streets of Istanbul to the tranquil shores of the Mediterranean, Turkey has woven a narrative that transcends time and beckons travellers with promises of discovery and delight. This concluding reflection seeks to encapsulate the diverse experiences and lasting memories that this enchanting country offers to every traveller.

1. Timeless Beauty of Istanbul: A Gateway to Two Continents

Your journey likely began in Istanbul, a city that effortlessly bridges the gap between Europe and Asia, reflecting a fusion of cultures, traditions, and histories. As you roamed through the historic districts of Sultanahmet and Beyoğlu, the Hagia Sophia and Blue Mosque stood as living testaments to the city's rich past, where Byzantine and Ottoman influences converge. The Grand Bazaar, with its labyrinthine alleys and vibrant stalls, invited you to immerse yourself in the art of negotiation and discovery.

Beyond the historical sites, the Bosphorus Strait, separating the European and Asian sides of Istanbul, became a conduit for both commerce and scenic beauty. A cruise along these azure waters revealed a cityscape that seamlessly integrates ancient minarets and palaces with modern skyscrapers, encapsulating the city's dynamic spirit.

In the evenings, Istanbul's vibrant nightlife beckoned, offering a kaleidoscope of experiences. From traditional meyhanes with lively music to rooftop bars with panoramic views, the city revealed its multifaceted character. The calls to prayer echoing from minarets intermingled with the laughter of locals and the chatter of fellow travellers, creating an atmosphere that resonated with the essence of Istanbul - a city where the past and present coexist harmoniously.

2. Historical Marvels: Ephesus and Beyond

As your journey took you beyond Istanbul, the ancient city of Ephesus unfolded like a chapter from a history book. The well-preserved ruins, from the Library of Celsus to the Terrace Houses, whispered tales of a bygone era. The Ephesus Archaeological Museum offered a deeper dive into the lives of those who once walked these streets, with artefacts providing glimpses into the daily rituals and grandeur of ancient Ephesians.

Venturing further, the journey led to Priene, Miletus, and Didyma, lesser-known but equally captivating ancient cities. The monumental Temple of Apollo in Didyma, the expansive theatre in Miletus, and the city planning marvel of Priene spoke to the advanced architectural and engineering prowess of the ancients.

Cappadocia, with its otherworldly landscapes, unfolded a different facet of Turkey's historical tapestry. The cave dwellings, fairy chimneys, and ancient cave churches in Göreme Open-Air Museum transported you to a surreal realm. Hot air balloon rides at sunrise provided a bird's-eye view of this unique landscape, creating memories that would linger long after the journey's end.

3. Outdoor Adventures: From Coast to Cave

For the adventure seekers, Turkey's diverse topography became a playground of thrilling experiences. In Antalya, white-water rafting on the Köprülü River infused adrenaline into the journey. The coastal town of Olympos, with its tree house accommodations, offered a rustic haven for relaxation after a day of adventure.

Paragliding over the azure waters of Ölüdeniz and canyoning in Saklikent Gorge near Fethiye elevated the journey to new heights, both literally and metaphorically. The tranquillity of Butterfly Valley, accessible only by boat, provided a serene contrast to the adrenaline-fueled activities.

Cappadocia's vast landscapes served as a canvas for outdoor escapades. ATV tours through valleys and hot air balloon rides at dawn allowed adventurers to connect with nature in exhilarating ways. Hiking in Ihlara Valley and exploring the underground cities revealed the region's geological wonders and ancient subterranean civilizations.

4. Coastal Retreat: Sun, Sea, and Serenity

For those seeking sun-soaked relaxation, the Mediterranean and Aegean coasts of Turkey unfolded like a series of tranquil retreats. In Bodrum, the blend of historical charm and maritime elegance set the stage for leisurely strolls along the marina and sunsets by the castle. A boat trip to Karaada Island's healing thermal waters became a therapeutic interlude in the coastal escape.

Kas, with its laid-back atmosphere and ancient ruins, provided a perfect backdrop for unhurried exploration. A boat trip to the Sunken City of Kekova and the ascent to Simena Castle offered both cultural and scenic delights. Kaputas Beach and Big Pebble Beach, nestled between steep cliffs, became havens of relaxation for those seeking the solace of sun and sea.

Antalya, the Mediterranean gem, invited travellers to delve into its ancient history while enjoying the modern comforts of seaside resorts. Exploring the Old Town, the ancient theatre of Perge, and the cascading Duden Waterfalls provided a harmonious blend of cultural discovery and natural beauty.

5. Gastronomic Pleasures: A Culinary Tapestry

Turkey's gastronomic scene became a highlight of your journey, a symphony of flavours that delighted the senses. Istanbul's Spice Bazaar set the stage, offering an aromatic introduction to the country's diverse culinary palette. Street food expeditions revealed the artistry of local vendors crafting simit, kebabs, and other delectable treats.

Gaziantep, recognized as the culinary capital of Turkey, presented a cornucopia of delights. Baklava tasting sessions, culinary walking tours, and visits to local markets allowed you to savour the region's renowned pistachios and rich culinary heritage. The city's hospitality mirrored the warmth of its kitchens, creating an immersive experience for every food enthusiast.

Throughout the journey, regional specialties unfolded on tables adorned with mezes, kebabs, fresh seafood, and the irresistible aroma of Turkish coffee. Cooking classes provided hands-on experiences, transforming travellers into culinary artists capable of recreating the flavours of Turkey in their own kitchens.

6. Cultural Immersion: Echoes of Tradition

As you traversed Turkey, the cultural tapestry woven by its people left an indelible mark. The warmth and hospitality of locals, evident in the traditional tea offerings and invitations into homes, embodied the essence of Turkish culture. Whether sharing stories with villagers in Cappadocia or partaking in Friday prayers in conservative regions, cultural immersion became a two-way exchange, fostering understanding and appreciation.

The vibrant bazaars and markets, where haggling is an art form, showcased the economic pulse of the country and offered glimpses into the daily lives of Turks. Traditional music and dance performances, whether in Istanbul or Cappadocia, revealed the rhythmic heartbeat of Turkey's cultural heritage.

Respecting local customs, dressing modestly when required, and adhering to religious site etiquettes became a testament to cultural sensitivity. The use of basic Turkish phrases, from greetings to expressions of gratitude, opened doors and hearts, creating bridges between diverse cultures.

7. A Tapestry of Memories: Navigating Turkey with Confidence

As you reflect on your journey through Turkey, it becomes apparent that each experience, whether historical, adventurous, leisurely, or culinary, has contributed to a tapestry of memories. Navigating the country with confidence involved not just traversing physical landscapes but also navigating cultural nuances and embracing the unknown with an open heart.

Health and safety considerations, from understanding local healthcare resources to respecting cultural norms, became integral components of the journey. Emergency preparedness, language considerations, and awareness of local customs enhanced your ability to immerse in the beauty and diversity of Turkey.

The architectural wonders of Istanbul, the ancient marvels of Ephesus, the adrenaline-filled adventures along the Turquoise Coast, the sun-soaked beaches, the gastronomic delights, and the cultural exchanges—all these elements intertwine to create a mosaic of experiences that define your journey through Turkey.

8. Farewell, but not Goodbye: A Heartfelt Adieu to Turkey

As you bid farewell to Turkey, you carry with you not just souvenirs and photographs but a collection of stories and emotions that will endure. The sights and sounds of bustling markets, the taste of baklava on your lips, the echoes of ancient prayers in historic mosques, and the warmth of Turkish hospitality—all these will linger in your heart, inviting you to return.

Turkey, with its multifaceted allure, has unveiled itself as a destination that transcends mere travel. It is an odyssey—a journey through time, landscapes, and cultures. It is an encounter—a meeting of past and present, tradition and modernity. It is an immersion—a plunge into the vibrant tapestry of Turkish life, where every thread, every colour, contributes to a story that is both unique and universally resonant.

In conclusion, your journey through Turkey has been a symphony, a dance, a feast, and an exploration—a journey to remember. As you step onto the plane, glance back at the land where East and West converge, where history is both ancient and alive, and where the embrace of culture is as warm as the Mediterranean sun. Turkey, with its enchanting allure, bids you a heartfelt adieu, with an unspoken invitation to return and rediscover the magic once again.

So, until we meet again on the crossroads of continents and cultures, carry these memories with you, let them inspire your dreams, and may the spirit of Turkey accompany you on your future adventures. A journey to remember—an odyssey that has left an indelible mark on your soul.

Don't miss out!

Visit the website below and you can sign up to receive emails whenever PA BOOKS publishes a new book. There's no charge and no obligation.

https://books2read.com/r/B-A-STTAB-JIGRC

BOOKS 2 READ

Connecting independent readers to independent writers.

Also by PA BOOKS

Hogan's Key
Kimberly & the Five Strange Goldfishes
The Enchanted Library
The Misadventures of Pirate Pete
From Wheel To Web: 40 Remarkable Inventions
Once Upon A Sleepy Time
The Global Game - The Evolution Of Football
Strides To Success: A Beginner's Guide to Running
The ChatGPT Handbook
Climate Crossroads
1000 Everyday Life Hacks
Urban Exploration - London The Comprehensive Travel Guide
Urban Exploration - New York The Comprehensive Travel Guide
Urban Exploration - Amsterdam The Comprehensive Travel Guide
Urban Exploration - Barcelona The Comprehensive Travel Guide
Urban Exploration - Dubai The Comprehensive Travel Guide
Urban Exploration - Paris The Comprehensive Travel Guide
World Of Festivals - The Ultimate Guide
The Ultimate Travellers Guide To Turkey

www.ingramcontent.com/pod-product-compliance
Ingram Content Group UK Ltd.
Pitfield, Milton Keynes, MK11 3LW, UK
UKHW011347100825
7319UKWH00021B/126